120 Greatest Anxiety Hacks

Some old, some new, and some truly unorthodox

Mel Bonthuys

All rights reserved

No part of this book may be used without written permission from the author.

This book is dedicated to every single person who has struggled with anxiety disorder.

May this book be a fun and entertaining addition to your recovery.

Disclaimers

Please take note of the following:

- The author in no way will accept any responsibility for any damage, illness or harm associated with following the advice in this book.
- It is a good idea to get checked out by a doctor before starting on any treatment plan.
- Never change/reduce or stop your medication without consulting with your doctor.
- Please be careful when taking herbal or natural remedies. Just because they are 'natural' doesn't mean they will necessarily agree with you. Always consult with a doctor or health professional as certain herbal remedies will counteract medication.
- The author is not a qualified psychologist, psychiatrist, doctor, pharmacist, nutritionist or exercise instructor. All opinions and/or advice from the author are to be carried out at the readers own risk. ☺
- If you are pregnant or suffer with any type of existing illness or even if you are in doubt about anything, please

consult with a doctor or health professional before undertaking any of the advice mentioned in this book.
- Make sure that you see a qualified, reputable and registered therapist and/or doctor before embarking on any kind of treatment plan or therapy.
- Never give up. Just because something works for one person, doesn't mean it will work for you, and just because something works for you doesn't mean it will work for the next person. It is about trial and error and finding what makes your life easier and more manageable. There is something out there that works for everyone, and you will find it! Most importantly though, fill your life with happy things and positive and uplifting moments. Try to not get involved in the negativities of life.
- This book is not a replacement for medication or therapy.
- All pictures are used with permission from the owners. Thank you, to all of you.
- Thank you to those people who allowed me to reference their work and share their links.

Table of Contents

Acknowledgements 15

Foreword 16

Section 1 – Hacks/Tips/Tricks/Techniques 21

    Positivity Tips 21

        Be Grateful 21

        Read Inspirational/Self Help Books 23

        Subscribe To Positive Websites or Text Message Services ... 25

        Motivational Videos 25

        Law Of Attraction 26

        Record I AM Affirmations 28

        Read Positive Testimonials 29

        Avoid Negative People 30

        Have Faith 33

        Pray 34

        Stick Positive Quotes Around Your House 36

        Wear An Elastic Band Around Your Wrist 37

        Fake Smile 37

    Writing and Doodling Techniques 40

        Scribble On A Piece Of Paper 40

Journaling / Writing Things Down 41

Write Something with Your Non-Dominant Hand 42

Exercise Recommendations 44

    Exercise 44

    Yoga 46

    Tai Chi 48

    Pilates 50

    Stretch The Neck 51

    Legs up the Wall 52

Inner Child Work 55

    Access The Inner Child 55

    Colour In 56

    Put Happy Stickers On Your Belongings 58

    Make a Picture Book 59

    Watch Cartoons 60

    Vision Board 61

    Calming Jars 61

Anger Management Hacks 64

    Count Backwards from 100 or Say the Alphabet Backwards 64

    Punch a Pillow 65

Scream Into a Pillow 66

Social Anxiety Hacks 67

    Listen To Calming Music Through Some Earphones When You're Out In Public 67

    Wear Sunglasses When You're Out in Public 67

    If You Struggle With Crowds, Go Out Early or Late Afternoon 68

    Smile At Someone 69

Eating and Diet Reminders 71

    Diet 71

    Eat Breakfast 77

    Herbal Tea Instead Of Caffeine 78

    Starch 82

    Anti-Stress Vitamins 83

    Anti-Stress Minerals 85

    Alcohol 86

Lifestyle Reminders 88

    Eliminate Chemicals 88

    Be Careful Of What You Read and Watch On TV 91

    Don't Watch Medical TV Programmes 92

Smoking 94

Keep Your Surroundings Clean 95

Get A Pet 96

Spring Clean 98

Force Your Hobbies 98

Natural Medicine Suggestions 103

St John's Wort 103

Rescue Remedy 103

Bach Flower Remedies 104

Breathing Exercises 107

Blow Up A Balloon 107

The 4-4-4-4 breath 108

The Candle Breath 109

The Five Senses Breath 111

Relaxation Hacks 113

Meditation 113

Aromatherapy 115

Balloon Stress Ball 119

Ground Yourself / Mindfulness 120

Massage and Pull Your Ears 121

Blow Cool Air Onto Your Thumb 122

Get A Desktop Zen Garden 123

Himalayan Salt Lamps 124

Popping Plastic 126

Reflex Points 127

The Naam Yoga Hand Trick 129

Colour Therapy 130

The 5-Minute Rule 133

Autonomous Sensory Meridian Response (ASMR) 135

Fractal Therapy 136

Psychology Methods and Therapies 138

Say Your Irrational Fears Out Loud 138

Be Your Own Psychologist 139

Emotional Freedom Technique (EFT) 142

The 'RAT' Method 144

Cognitive Behavioural Therapy (CBT) 147

Schedule Time To Worry 148

Interesting Extras and Important Information! 152

Psychodynamic Therapy 153

Gestalt Therapy 154

Biofeedback 155

Magnet Therapy 156

Hypnotherapy 156

Tremor Release Exercise 157

Noise Tips 159

Noise 159

Music 161

Pink, White and Brown Noise 162

Time Management Tips 165

Planning Ahead / Routines 165

Adopt The 'Slow Down' Rule 167

Tips for Stigma and Dealing with Shame 170

Know That You Are Not Insane 170

Don't Be Ashamed 171

Getting To Grips With Your Anxiety 173

Admit When You're Feeling Down 173

Accept Your Anxiety 175

Know Your Triggers 177

Investigate and Research 178

Name Your Anxiety 180

Making Life Easier 181

    Survival Toolbox 181

    Recovery Toolbox 182

    Get A Support Structure 183

    Think About The Big In The Small Term 185

    Learn To Say No 186

    Keep It Simple 188

    Occupy The Mind 189

    Stay In The Moment 190

Sleep Tricks 193

    Weighted Blankets 196

    Do Not Nap For More Than 45 Minutes 197

Helping Others To Help You 200

    Talk It Out 200

    Donate Your Time 201

The Best Things In Life Are Free 203

    Laughter Is Truly The Best Medicine 203

    Give Yourself Me Time 204

    Spread Love 206

    Nature 206

Water Tricks 209

    Hold An Ice Block When You Feel A Panic Attack Coming On 209

    Suck On Ice Cubes Or Frozen Vegetables 210

    Cold Water Shocker 211

    Wash Your Hands In Warm Water 212

Challenge Yourself 214

    Do Something You've Always Wanted To Do, But Have Been Too Scared 214

Section 2 – Helpful Resources 216

    Facebook Pages: 216

    Books: 216

    Anxiety Support Centres: 217

Section 3 – References and links 218

About the Author: 226

    Other Books by Author 227

Acknowledgements

I would like to thank each and every photographer who allowed me to use their photographs in this book.

I would like to thank everyone who allowed me to reference their work, links or products.

Foreword

Ten years ago, mental illness was a very taboo subject.

No one really knew much about them, but fast forward to the current times, and mental illness is a hot topic, with more and more people speaking out about mental illness and creating awareness in an effort to stop the stigma associated with them.

However, it's still not enough!

There is still a stigma, and there are still many people suffering in silence!

Why do people suffer in silence?

It's because each and every person that struggles with a mental illness has different circumstances, and those circumstances make a huge difference when it comes to recovery.

Sometimes you will get people whose circumstances force them to suffer alone, because of mockery from someone they know, and now they are too scared and ashamed to ask for any help. Some people don't have any support from their family and get told it's all in their head and they must stop being 'weak', and then there are some people, like me, who are extremely lucky to have the people in my life that I do, that totally helped me each and every step of the way. They never judged me and were basically my rock when I needed them to be.

Since being struck down with my first ever anxiety attack in 2001, I have gone through a whirlwind of emotions, setbacks, and victories with my anxiety disorder.

If you read my first book 'My Anxiety Companion', you would have read all about my own personal story with my anxiety and how, throughout all these years, I have dedicated much of my time to 'trying and testing' just about every tip, hack, hint, strategy, method, programme, medication and piece of advice that is out there.

Throughout the trials and errors, I really have come to love, and ultimately rely on, many tips and hacks to help me get through my bad days.

Some of these tips are the golden old classics and are very well known. Some of them you may not have heard of before, and some of them are well...plain weird...but every single one of these tips that I have mentioned in this book are ones that I have personally found to work and ones that I use myself.

I have, however, also included a couple of techniques that I have not tried myself but that come with a great deal of praise or evidence of working well, and I have listed them in this book so that you can have a vast amount of different techniques, hacks and tips available to you, and it is up to you to find out which works best for you. So, I have mentioned a few of them, and maybe just maybe, one of them might be your saving grace? Who knows? ;)

In all honesty though, I know how debilitating it can be to feel like you are having a boxing match with your own mind every single day.

I also know what it's like to be so anxious that you don't know if you'll ever recover or be in a state of 'normalcy' again, and I promise you that these tips are what has gotten me through some of my worst of days.

It is important to remember though, that this book is not a substitute for any medication or therapy, and in order to really get on the road to recovery, you must understand that there are many different angles that need to be addressed in order to recover from anxiety disorder.

Thought patterns, changing negative habits and beliefs, and being able to control intrusive thoughts require a lot of patience, strength and determination, and you'll get there if you persevere!

I have also learned that by changing certain things within my life - and making them a habit, a person can find hope, happiness and acceptance inside oneself.

Finally, after many years of suffering, I see beauty again and I feel positive about life.

I want everyone out there to know that recovery takes time. We all respond to different things, but while you are recovering - like me, I want you to know that it is still possible to live a very fulfilling and happy life!

This is my hope for you as well, and I dedicate this book to all of you reading this.

May this book be of great use to you and provide you with support, reassurance, and be a stepping stone towards your ultimate recovery!

I have designed this book in a very fun and easy to read format. I didn't want this to be a typical, lengthy 'self-help' read, but rather short and 'straight to the point' tips and ideas that are quick and easy to refer to.

Each and every tip is categorized into a group, making it more accessible in time of need.

All tips, hacks and tricks have a how and why explanation to go with them, and a few of them even have some interesting scientific information for you to read through!

This book also includes a picture every so often to make the book more visually appealing, easier to use, and to give the book more of a 'child-like' feel.

I hope you enjoy this book as much as I enjoyed putting it together!

Yours in recovery,

Mel xxx

Section 1 – Hacks/Tips/Tricks/Techniques

Positivity Tips

Be Grateful

I have had to adopt certain changes into my life and make them a habit in order to make life better and easier for myself and this technique is one of them!

This simple but highly effective technique has had such a profound impact on my life that I cannot recommend it enough. I have experienced nothing but benefits since doing this.

Every single morning when you wake up, before you even get out of bed, say something you are grateful for. In fact, you don't even have to stipulate anything specific that you are thankful for, just by saying 'thank you' you are expressing gratitude.

Going through your day to day activities, every time something good happens to you, say 'thank you'. Maybe you pulled into a great parking space or maybe you got a free drink with lunch, no matter how small the good things seem – just say thank you!

Something that I do is I say 'thank you for hot water' when I'm showering or bathing as I remember those who don't have that luxury. Sometimes when loading my dishwasher, I give thanks for having the luxury of having something that makes my life easier.

Why express gratitude every day?

- When we express gratitude, we attract more abundance.
- We remain humble.
- It helps us to remember that even though we struggle with mental illness, there is always someone struggling with something far worse.
- It keeps the ego down.
- It teaches us to be more positive.
- It helps us to see that there is always something to be thankful for.

SIDE NOTE: It can be hard to express gratitude when you feel so down and out, so I then recommend focusing on the very small things that you have in your life that maybe someone else doesn't – after all, isn't that the whole point of being grateful? Being grateful for something as simple as having a roof over your head or having someone to support you in your time of need can make a big difference, and it will help you focus on the positive things that you have instead of your mental illness.

You don't even need to be grateful for something specific - just say 'thank you'

SIMPLE!

Read Inspirational/Self Help Books

A little tip from a motivational speaker I was once listening to, was to read something every day.

However, this didn't apply to fictional novels!

It applied to reading motivational and inspirational books.

I try to read something inspirational every day.

Of course, this doesn't mean that I don't read novels, but I really encourage you to start reading biographies and self-help books. One book I absolutely love is Rhonda Byrne's 'The Secret' which I'm quite sure you have all heard of, if not read.

Another thing the speaker said that has stuck in my mind is that whatever we read before we go to sleep will determine our dreams and state of mind when we sleep. That spoke to me and it should for you as well.

Try to read something light hearted or positive before your head hits the pillow, even if it's just a couple of pages – fill yourself with happiness and inspiring words!

Image credit: Pixabay/Congerdesign

Some ideas that you can try are:

- Rhonda Byrne's series of books.
- Chicken Soup for the soul series of books.
- Any book on how to develop a new skill.
- Any self-help book that helps you to better yourself.

SIDE NOTE: *If you are not much of a reader – then I have the perfect solution for you! Opt to listen to motivational speeches. There are hundreds of them on YouTube that range from short 3-minute inspirations to 2-hour talks. Another idea to try are the audible books where you listen to someone narrating the book to you.*

Subscribe To Positive Websites or Text Message Services

I honestly don't understand why more people don't do this.

These make such a difference especially if you are one of those people who doesn't really have a strong support system.

Once signed up, you will receive something positive to read and sometimes they can come just at the right time when you really need to hear them!

This can be done through a website or text message.

Motivational Videos

This is something that I have only recently discovered and they are very easily accessible on YouTube.

These videos really have a knack of building your self-esteem and making you feel so inspired.

Even if I am having a bad day, they just give me that nudge that I need to get out of my dark place and get some of my hope back.

Law Of Attraction

I keep bringing the Law of Attraction up because I truly believe that it makes a big difference in our lives.

It has made a profound difference in mine and has contributed a lot to much of my recovery. Almost all of us have heard 'what goes around comes around' or 'you reap what you sow.'

We are energy beings in a physical human body, meaning we have got to acknowledge that we have physical, mental and spiritual parts of us.

The spiritual part of us relates to everything that we attract, because as mentioned before, everything is made of energy, from us as human beings, to nature, to animals, right down to the pencils sitting on my desk.

Whether you believe in it or not doesn't matter. What does matter is that you believe in positivity over negativity, laughter over sadness and gratitude over complaining.

If you want to start attracting more of the good things into your life instead of the bad things, then you have to put in the work!

The most amazing thing about this is it needn't be happening or even be real. That's the beauty of the law of attraction, you get to make believe and pretend that everything is how you want it to be – and then one day, you actually start to believe it yourself, and then after that, things actually start changing!

It sounds too good to be true, but I'm telling you this because I have experienced the law of attraction and how it works more than once in my life, and since using it and focusing only on the positive, I am just reaping and reaping the benefits!

If you are sad – that is absolutely fine. No one is saying you must be happy every day, but on your sad or bad days, leave your manifestation work until the next day. Choose to be gentle with yourself, surround yourself with positive things and take the focus off of anything that will contribute to your sadness, and believe that you will be better the next day!

I promise you with all of my heart that this stuff works, but you must believe it and more importantly believe that you deserve better, and I promise you that your life and your anxiety will be so much better when you start applying positivity, gratitude and the law of attraction into it!

See the tip on 'Be Grateful' for more on this and get Rhonda Byrne's book 'The Secret' if you haven't already!

Record I AM Affirmations

I AM affirmations are positive and uplifting statements that are designed for you to listen to and repeat so that your brain actually believes them!

You can listen to so many of these affirmations on YouTube, but I find it better to actually record my own so that when I listen to them I hear my own voice – it somehow makes it more believable.

Some examples of these affirmations include:

- I am enough
- I am safe
- I am a success
- I am deserving

If you're focusing on achieving a dream or goal, say an affirmation for it - pretend that it's already come true! That is the key! Say for example, your dream is to qualify as a psychologist and run your own practice, your affirmations could be something like, "I am a qualified psychologist," and, "I have my own psychology practice."

If you don't want to listen to recordings, then write down your Affirmations and put them in a place where you'll always see them, such as on the wall by your computer, or on the mirror so that when you're getting ready you can see them.

Say them over and over again so that it goes through into the subconscious part of your brain!

Read Positive Testimonials

There is nothing more empowering than reading someone's story of success.

When I was at my worst with my anxiety, reading other people's success stories really helped inspire me and encourage me to want to recover.

They don't even need to be stories about mental health. Reading anything that describes a person's struggle to success is extremely inspiring!

Believe it or not, sometimes when you are so deep in the depths of despair, you actually start believing that you will never feel good again, and to make matters worse, you actually start giving up to the point where you don't have the energy or inspiration to try and get better.

It happens to the best of us and this is where these kinds of stories of inspiration can really work wonders. They immediately provide encouragement and hope and will help you to see that you can, and deserve to, feel better!

Call it a small 'glimmer of hope.'

Avoid Negative People

Toxic people are like vampires who literally suck all the goodness out of life.

These are the people who are always negative, they're always moaning and they just bug us to the degree that we start to take on their energy.

Actually, these people are called psychic vampires!

Unfortunately, this can be true for people who we consider friends. It's a hard one because it involves letting go, and that is not easy to do, especially if it's someone in your life whom you have had a lot to do with.

However, you need to stay away from, or else limit your time around, these types of people.

Most of the time, they are not even aware that they are having such a negative effect on others.

It doesn't make them a bad person, it is just how they have grown up. However, they are emotionally draining, and unless you know how to not take on that negativity, it is best to avoid them.

People with anxiety are very sensitive and we can be easily affected by people and things around us, so keeping these kinds of people at arm's length is very important for our mental health.

If it's someone who is not a friend, who doesn't really mean that much to you or your life, then it's a lot easier to distance yourself until the 'acquaintance' with that person just eventually fizzles out, but what if they are special to you? What if they are a friend? You obviously don't want to hurt their feelings. So how do you handle it?

Here are some tips to make this a bit easier:

- Whenever they start talking about something negative – immediately change the subject to something happier, funnier or positive.
- Try to not ask questions about bad stuff that is happening in their life. Keep the conversation light hearted and ask them questions that you know will be answered positively. Such as, "How delicious was that food that we ate the other day?"
- Do not respond at all to their negative commentary. Listen to what they have to say, but as soon as you stop commenting on their negative talk, they will eventually realize that they not going to get a reaction out of you anymore.
- Make a point to highlight something positive when you see them. Say things such as "Wow, what a beautiful day it is," or, "Your hair looks amazing today."
- Try to maybe not spend as much time with them. Make an excuse to cut your visit short.
- Send them an email with a link to one of the many positive and inspirational videos that are on YouTube and tell them how amazing it made you feel.

Have Faith

Before I go any further with this particular point, I just want to emphasize that the 'faith' I am talking about has to do with believing in oneself and has no religious connotations attached to it whatsoever.

I have always thought of faith as being one of the most beautiful things that a person can have, and it's for two reasons:

Firstly, faith is the opposite of fear, which should already speak volumes to you and secondly, to have faith is to believe in something that you cannot see.

Believing that something will work out or happen the way you want it to, and by doing this purely on blind faith, just knocks the anxiety right out of the way, because you're putting your energy into it - your heart and soul!

Fear is also something you cannot see, so when we replace the fear with faith, we change our feelings from 'nothing to live for' to 'something to live for', we change from nothing to believe in to something to believe in.

Most of all, we change our feelings from negative to positive.

Of course, this is easier said than done.

Changing your fear into faith is one of the most difficult things I have ever had to do, and I'm still working on it myself.

However here are a few things that have helped me so far:

- Accepting my Anxiety Disorder for what it is.
- Counting my blessings.
- Practicing self-care. This helps a person to see that they are deserving of happiness.
- Realizing and believing that I am deserving of love and happiness.
- Reading 'The Secret' – seriously just go read the book!

Pray

Again, I need to emphasize that I am not focusing on religion here or any specific religion. I am merely pointing out what has helped me in my recovery.

First of all, let me tell you something right now:

I don't even believe that you need to be religious or follow one particular path in order to feel the benefits of prayer. I am not a religious person at all, and I have felt amazing benefits from the power of prayer, because it's all to do with intent!

This may come as a shock to a lot of you, especially since we think of prayer as kneeling, with our hands in a prayer position, and praying to God. However, did you even know that by just saying the words 'Thank you' that you are in fact praying? What about when we sing happy birthday to someone and they blow out the candles on their cake and then they make a wish? Is that not also praying? What about when we say silently to ourselves "I hope this works – please let this work" Is that not a prayer?

This is what people fail to realize.

It is not about who or what or how you are praying. It is not about fancy words and long speeches, and it certainly is not about being religious. It is merely taking the time to be grateful for all that you have in your life, or else to ask for assistance from whoever you perceive as your God, the universe, higher being, source, or deity – whatever comes naturally to you!

Again, it's about intent! It's about what you feel in your heart!

A lot of us just speak to the air or the universe, because no matter what you think, every single word you say is 'putting it out there' into the world and leaving its mark.

That is why I am always saying to you guys to always say what you're thankful for — because it's putting something positive out into the universe!

Stick Positive Quotes Around Your House

How awesome is this? I love this neat trick!

I have made a point of sticking short positive quotes all around my house. One is on my mirror, one is on my fridge, and I have many of them covering the walls of my study! I even have one in the bathroom cabinet, so when I'm brushing my teeth, I am forced to look at it.

I find that surrounding myself and bombarding my mind with these constant positive messages and quotes, I don't have time to think of the negative.

When I'm busy at my computer, and I get side tracked, I will often find myself daydreaming and staring at all my positive quotes that I have stuck on the wall above my computer!

Wear An Elastic Band Around Your Wrist

This was a weird one for me, but my word, does this work like a charm!

The object is to wear an elastic band (an ordinary hair tie or stretchy bracelet will do) around your wrist and every time you think or say something negative, snap the band against your wrist.

It is a very good technique this one!

I use it often because I always have hair ties around my wrists in case I want to tie my hair up, so it makes it a very easy and 'at your fingertips' kind of hack!

I have been able to actually stop myself before I say something that is either negative or hateful, and I'm convinced it's because of a combination of this technique and listening to the motivational videos.

Fake Smile

One of my most recent favourite anxiety hacks!

I've been doing this all the time, especially when I'm on my own.

Seriously, you have to try this one!

Quite a while ago when I wasn't feeling my best, I decided to just smile in spite of what I was feeling!

What I felt afterwards was phenomenal.

My mood instantly lifted, I felt more inspired and even energized!

So now when I feel stressed or sad, I actually smile – a big toothy smile and I promise you it works!

This hack is actually backed by research and various experiments have been done, which show that smiling, even when a person is stressed or sad, can make them feel better.

Why does this happen?

It is not fully understood, but it has been suggested that smiling - even fake smiling could reduce cortisol levels in the body.

As human beings, we also associate smiling with happiness, so perhaps it could be purely psychological?

Smiling is also said to increase our feel-good hormones like endorphins.

So, whatever the reason as to why smiling makes us feel better, give it a try and see for yourself!

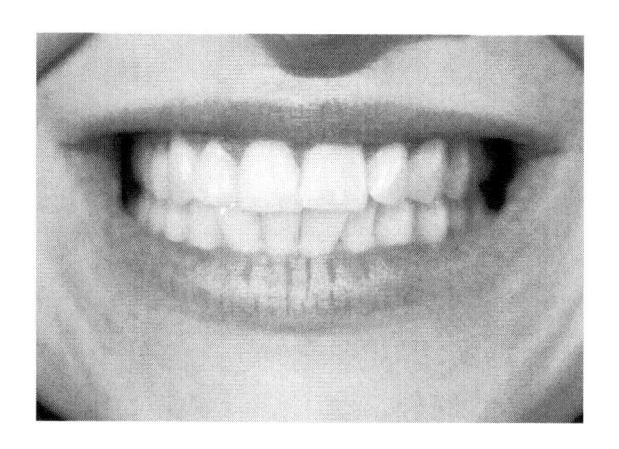

Image credit: Pixabay/Kjerstin_Michaela

Writing and Doodling Techniques

Scribble On A Piece Of Paper

This is a great anger management technique.

Get a piece of cardboard or paper or whatever you have lying around. The bigger the more benefit it will be. Take a pen or pencil and just scribble and let your mood guide you as to how hard, softly, or quickly you scribble.

Let all your frustrations out onto the page.

Draw or scribble whatever comes to mind and use whichever colour you feel like using.

If you are angry, you may choose to use black and scribble very hard, whereas if you are feeling happy, you may want to use a blue colour with lighter strokes.

SIDE NOTE: *Keep a scribble diary and compare your doodles/drawings and scribbles over a week and see if they differ at all depending on your mood.*

Journaling / Writing Things Down

This tip brings back memories of my teenage years where I, like many other girls, would keep a diary with one of those lock and keys. It was here that all my thoughts and frustrations about school and teenage life could be expressed, and even though it was like talking to a brick wall, for some reason, it made me feel better.

Expressing your thoughts down on paper is very therapeutic, and for me personally, it's what started my first book. It's the middle ground between thinking something and voicing something, and it's very personal.

When you write your feelings down, it's kind of like 'casting them in stone' because it's not a thought or a voiced opinion that can be forgotten the next day. It's always there and can be re-read whenever you need to.

Also, for me, writing down my feelings as opposed to just thinking them or saying them is somehow stronger.

All you need for this is a blank notebook and a pen or pencil and start writing down how you are feeling. You'll be amazed at what comes out, and sometimes you are even able to see a pattern forming of how and when certain emotions come up.

The great thing about journaling is there is no right or wrong.

It's your personal space to write out your inner most thoughts and feelings that are for your eyes only!

Image credit: Author's own

Write Something with Your Non-Dominant Hand

The next time you feel anxious or panicky, try this really cool trick!

Grab a pen and start writing, but with your non-dominant hand!

I would also strongly recommend writing calming words such as 'relaxation' or 'I am safe'.

There are a few reasons for this, but first the science of it:

The brain needs exercise to keep it sharp, and you can do this through mental stimulation.

When you do something with your non-dominant hand, such as writing, the brain, which relies on everything that it has learned through the years, gets confused, as it's not used to doing things with the non-dominant hand. This brings about lots of creativity within the brain.

Also, when we use our dominant hand, only one hemisphere is activated, however, when using your non-dominant hand, both hemispheres are activated, thus helping to integrate the two hemispheres.

So how does this help anxiety?

First of all, because you're doing something you are not used to doing, it requires more focus and concentration, therefore, taking the mind off anxiety and disruptive thought patterns that may come about.

Secondly, as I suggested, perhaps write down calming words as this will further enhance feelings of relaxation.

Exercise Recommendations

Exercise

Before I get into some great exercises that I personally find great for anxiety, let's talk about why you should be moving your body, and before you roll your eyes, here's a fun fact for you:

Did you know that without regular exercise, 18 hormones made by the body cannot work properly? This is a bad thing because the endocrine system and our hormones play a vital role in keeping our nervous systems functioning well.

If that didn't inspire you to start exercising, then I don't know what will, because it's that little fact that echoes in my head each time I don't feel like exercising and I'm telling you it inspires me to get my body moving.

I am fully aware that some people don't enjoy exercising. My mother is one of those people and the trick to combating this is to find something you enjoy.

It's no point doing something that you don't like, because then it becomes a chore rather than an enjoyable activity.

I also find that making exercise part of your daily 'transport' helps a lot. If you need to get somewhere then opt to walk or ride your bike (obviously within reason.) Whenever I go up to the shop, I deliberately take the long way through the park and by the time I have gone to the shop and walked back home, I have walked for 30 minutes, and that's my exercise done for the day.

You don't need to belong to a gym, and as far as I am concerned, saying that you don't belong to or can't afford a gym is just an excuse! Unless you are disabled or in a wheelchair, you have two legs – so get up and WALK! Also, with all the great online videos and apps – there really is no excuse guys!

For me personally, I enjoy walking in the woods or a park and I also love cycling.

Another exercise I love, as you all know, is yoga, and more recently I've been enjoying weight training with a very light set of dumbbells.

Please also don't forget that exercise releases endorphins, which are another set of hormones which make you happy and also act as a natural analgesic (pain reliever.)

Yoga

I am quite sure by now that most of you have heard of using yoga as a stress reliever, so I'm not going to go into it deeply. There are many books and information on yoga and I do encourage you to read up on this amazing practice.

However, if you don't know much about yoga, in a nutshell, yoga aims to unify the mind and body. So, when you do yoga, you are trying to balance the mind, body and spirit and make them one. It is believed that in order for the mind, body and spirit to be healthy and work properly, they have to be in harmony with one another.

It takes you through a series of beautiful poses (known as asanas) and breaths (known as prana), gently stretching the muscles and using the breath to achieve the desired pose.

Yoga helps and improves a variety of different things both physically and mentally, including but not limited to:

- It helps us to use our lungs and cardiovascular system more efficiently.
- It helps us to breathe correctly.

- It allows more energy to flow through freely.
- It increases flexibility and suppleness.
- It improves balance and coordination.
- It maintains bone density.
- It is safe: due to the slow pace in which the poses are performed, and the focus that is needed, it is very unlikely that you will hurt yourself.
- It tones the body and trims fat.
- It teaches correct posture.
- It lengthens and strengthens the body.
- It teaches us to use our core strength (stomach) for most asanas, which helps to protect the back against injury.
- It increases our ability to relax.
- It improves our sleep patterns.
- It improves concentration and focus.
- It reduces depression and anxiety.

Recently I did a 30-day yoga challenge and I honestly thought I would cave by day 10, but surprisingly I actually didn't and I thoroughly enjoyed doing the practice every morning. I learned that by exercising in the morning I am more alert and grounded throughout my day, and when I followed yoga with a meditation, I felt even calmer.

It's just not possible for me to not praise this beautiful practice.

SIDE NOTE 1: Even though numerous videos of yoga can be found online, it is always advisable to join a class with a qualified Yoga instructor especially if you have never done it before.

SIDE NOTE 2: Always be aware of contra-indications and let the instructor known of any injuries or concerns. Certain poses must also be avoided if you are menstruating or pregnant.

Image credit: Pixabay/Irina Logra

Tai Chi

Tai Chi is one of the many Chinese martial arts that use a combination of very slow and precise movements along with breathing to bring out relaxation. Due to the fact that it is done at a very slow pace and it is a low impact exercise, it is highly unlikely to cause injury, thus making it suitable for people of all ages.

Tai Chi has been called 'meditation in motion' because of the slow and meditative manner in which the moves are performed. This makes it an excellent practice for anxiety and stress reduction. It also helps improve concentration, posture and strength in the legs.

It has even been said to reduce falls in the elderly.

Tai Chi is very relative to 'Chi' which is the vital energy source within all of us. It is believed that if one of these energy pathways, known as meridians are blocked, then illness can form, whether it physical or mental.

Some different types of Tai Chi include Chen, Yan, and Wu, with speed and holding of the poses being the main differences between them.

SIDE NOTE 1: *It is always advisable to join a class with a qualified Tai Chi instructor.*

SIDE NOTE 2: *Although injury is unlikely, always let the instructor known of any injuries, concerns, or if you are pregnant.*

Pilates

Pilates was founded by Joseph Pilates in the 1900's and like Yoga and Tai Chi, is also a mind and body combination of exercises.

It focuses on using the core (stomach) to achieve a series of repetitive stretching and strengthening exercises, while also focusing a lot on breath.

By using the core to perform all the hard work, the back is automatically protected.

Pilates is also a low impact form of exercise and therefore suitable for people of all ages.

One of the things I must highlight with Pilates is how aware I became of my breathing and it was here that I learned to breathe properly.

There are so many books on Pilates as well as online videos that can be accessed, but I advise going to a qualified instructor if you are a beginner.

SIDE NOTE 1: *It is always advisable to join a class with a qualified Pilates instructor.*

SIDE NOTE 2: *Although injury is unlikely, always let the instructor known of any injuries, concerns, or if you are pregnant.*

Stretch The Neck

Doing neck exercises won't help to reduce anxiety as such, but it will help to reduce tension headaches caused by stress and anxiety.

I find it to be of great benefit when done before going to bed and then again in the morning before getting up.

This will help reduce those tension headaches and would be great for someone who suffers with migraines or frequent headaches caused by stress - or even if you sit at the computer a lot.

We all have what is known as the 'trapezius' area at the back of our necks, extending across each shoulder and down the back just between and at the top of the shoulder blades, making the shape of an upside-down triangle.

This is the area where all our stress is carried.

By doing neck stretches and exercises, we can help to dispel some of this tension.

Three of my favourite neck exercises include:

Side to Side – Sit or stand up straight, breathe in and look straight ahead, breathe out and look to your left. Breathe in and bring your head back to centre. Breathe out and look to your right. Repeat as many times as you like until your neck feels better.

Half-Moon – Gently drop your chin to your chest and roll your head in a half circle from left to right. Bring your head upright and then drop it back so that you can see the ceiling. Roll your head from left to right. Return to a normal upright position.

Arm Neck Stretch – This one is my personal favourite. Bring your right arm over your head to your left ear and gently pull your head to the right side. Stretch your left arm out to the side. You will feel a deep stretch in the left side of your neck and down your left arm. Repeat on the other side.

Legs up the Wall

I seriously love this pose!

This is actually a yoga pose and is one of the most relaxing and grounding poses I've come across.

All you do is lie with your butt against the wall, back flat on the floor, and put your legs up against the wall so your feet are in the air.

You can place a blanket under your lower back if you wish, or you can use blocks under your hips.

This will help to relieve lower back pressure.

Back when I went to yoga classes, we would place one of those big yoga balls on our feet, and it was surprisingly very peaceful. You couldn't even feel the weight of the ball!

Combine this pose with deep breathing and you'll experience a calmer nervous system and a clearer mind.

I would even add some soft music, put a small towel over my eyes, and hold this position for 5-10 minutes.

When you feel stressed over your work load – go and do this pose.

If you're in an open office environment, then obviously you can't exactly go and put your legs up the wall, but if you are able to, and you are on your own, try this pose!

SIDE NOTE: *Girls, please don't do this pose if you are menstruating! Please also check before doing this pose if you are pregnant!*

Inner Child Work

Access The Inner Child

Our inner child is just screaming to have a little TLC and in these times of major stress and busy schedules, nourishing the inner child has never been more important!

Over the past year or so, there has been a lot of talk about accessing the inner child and in particular, adult colouring in.

At first glance, it may seem silly, but it's vitally important that we understand why we need to give ourselves some 'child' time.

As adults we have completely lost the ability to be child-like for fear of it being immature. However, studies are proving just how important it is to practice inner child work. It releases stress, improves concentration and allows us to put away the harsh reality of the world for a few hours.

Here are some ideas on how to access the inner child:

- Colouring in a colouring book
- Go to the park and swing on a swing
- Read a book from your childhood

- Roll around on the grass
- Watch a cartoon
- Run through a sprinkler
- Fly a kite
- Blow bubbles
- Paint
- Listen to nursery rhymes
- If you've kept toys from your childhood, get them out and reminisce
- Get out your baby photo album and remember old times
- Build a jigsaw puzzle
- Go to a toy store

If you are interested in the adult colouring books, like so many people are, there are a wide variety of books available with different themes and designs. You can purchase them at most book shops and stationary stores, or else online.

See more on adult 'colouring in' on the next tip.

Colour In

This is a form of inner child work and colour therapy.

Don't brush this off as being silly or something that only children do!

It has proved very popular recently, with everyone wanting to try it out and bookstores selling just about every theme you can think of.

Of course, you can just buy a child's colouring book, but adult colouring books are so much more challenging because the pictures are a lot more detailed and busy.

They have been specifically designed so you can use maximum concentration.

Here are some reasons why I love colouring in:

It nurtures the inner child – Most of us had colouring books as children, and this is why it recaptures that inner child within us. We are living in an age where our lifestyles are very rushed and stressed and we all forget that there is an inner child inside us needing some nurturing, and colouring is a great way to do it.

Colour Therapy - I speak about this more in the tip on colour therapy but for me though, colour makes me happy and lifts my mood, and seeing my finished picture in all different colours helps me achieve a happier mood.

Improved concentration and focus - Colouring requires concentration and focus, and this is what makes it therapeutic. Combine that with heaps of divine colours and you really have an amazing tool for stress and anxiety relief.

Image credit: Pixabay/the3cats

Put Happy Stickers On Your Belongings

I know this may seem pointless, but it seriously works!

I bought some little stickers with smiley faces on them, and I have stuck them on things that I am bound to see or touch throughout the day. I have one on my keychain, my phone, my computer and my I-pad.

The idea is that every time you see one of these stickers, you are reminded to smile and be positive. Although quite frankly, because it is such a strange hack, I just end up laughing when I see them which is even better!

You can get any kind of stickers that you want.

Perhaps something that makes you smile.

So, if you like butterflies, try to get some butterfly stickers. The size, colour and image of the stickers don't matter, as long as it will remind you to be happy.

Make a Picture Book

I started doing this a couple of years ago and now I have two picture books.

All you have to do is buy a notebook or journal and print out or cut out pictures from magazines and stick them in the book.

The pictures should be of things that make you feel happy and at peace, so when you feel sad or just need a pick me up, you can page through this book.

Some of the pictures in my book consist of:

- Animals
- Nature
- Pretty houses
- Beaches
- Inspiring words or quotations
- Countryside scenes
- Flowers

Watch Cartoons

Just admit it! You love watching cartoons!

It's something we never really grow out of, even if we don't like to admit it.

This is possibly one of my favourite inner child techniques ever.

What I love about cartoons is the world they live in. I love the innocence and I love how even if you 'die' in the cartoon world, you seem to magically come back to life!! ☺

It's such a refreshing break from reality.

Vision Board

This is a truly wonderful idea to help visualize what you want your future to look like.

Making a vision board is also very therapeutic.

Simply cut out pictures that resonate to your goals and dreams that you want to achieve and paste them onto a big sheet of cardboard.

Stick it up where you will always see it. By doing this, you will be forcing yourself and your mind to focus on what you truly want in life and for your future. It will encourage you to start taking more action towards your goals and it will keep you positive throughout your day.

I have my vision board stuck up right above my computer in my study, so that I am always looking at it throughout the day.

Calming Jars

These are so easy and therapeutic to make, they look attractive in the home and they help to alleviate stress.

There are many different ones that you can make and you can get creative as well.

The most basic one and the one I love the most is the one with glitter.

All you need for this is a clean empty jar, water, glitter glue or some clear glue, food colouring and some glitter. A mason jar with a screw lid is best.

If you have children around the house – maybe opt for a plastic jar.

Fill your jar with hot water, add in the bottle of glitter glue and stir it.

Finally add in some food colouring.

Then add in the glitter and stir it again. Seal it tightly (you can even glue it).

The idea is to then shake the bottle and watch the glitter fall to the bottom.

Again, I have two that I have made and I keep them in my study, and when I feel like taking a breather, I shake the bottles and look at my vision board!

There are plenty of blogs and videos where you can watch and get some awesome ideas.

I also strongly suggest checking out this blog for 11 awesome different calm down jars!

http://www.therealisticmama.com/11-awesome-calm-down-jars/

Image credit: Author's own

Anger Management Hacks

Count Backwards from 100 or Say the Alphabet Backwards

I have included these in the same point because they will both have the same effect.

I remember very clearly one day, I was very frustrated at work. A client was there and saw my frustration and said to me, "It's ok Mel, just count backwards from 100."

This got me thinking and very often to take my mind off of something, I do count backwards.

Here is how it can help you:

- This will help you to focus on the numbers or letters instead of your anxiety or panic.
- By saying or counting the numbers or letters backwards, it forces you to concentrate, therefore diverting your attention.

- If you can, try and picture the numbers or letters in your head to focus your attention even more.

SIDE NOTE: *My husband swears by this technique for when he can't sleep!*

Punch a Pillow

Yes, you did read that correctly! ☺

This is a great anger relieving technique. It sure beats putting a hole through the wall, plus you will get an added workout!

So, grab a fluffy pillow and practice your punches on that.

SIDE NOTE: *Something even better would be to invest in a punching bag. If you find you have trouble controlling your anger and get into heated conversations a lot of the time, then this really will help you!*

Scream Into a Pillow

Ever heard of the expression, "I feel as though I'm going to scream."

I have no idea why, but this works so well! Just to be able to vent all your built-up frustration into something that can't judge or back chat you!

Screaming into a pillow is almost like having a good cry.

It just releases all that tension, and the sound is very muffled, so no one will hear you!

Try combining this with punching a pillow - great combo!

Social Anxiety Hacks

Listen To Calming Music Through Some Earphones When You're Out In Public

This is one of my most favourite social anxiety tips ever.

By having earphones on, you are able to drown out the noise of the outside world. This enables you to almost be 'locked' in your own world and mind, creating a calming atmosphere.

It seriously works! Trust me – I do this all the time!

Wear Sunglasses When You're Out in Public

I have done a couple of YouTube videos on this, but this is another of my favourite social anxiety tips.

People with anxiety, especially social anxiety, do not want to be seen or focused on and this is where this trick works like a charm.

It creates an 'if you can't see me, then I can't see you' feeling.

Combine this with the above tip and you'll be sorted if you don't like going out in public.

Image Credit: Pixabay/webandi

If You Struggle With Crowds, Go Out Early or Late Afternoon

Honestly, I loathe crowds, I cannot handle crowds.

If you want me to have an immediate panic attack, then take me into a huge crowd of people!

It sends my panic meter into overdrive! I find I get extremely claustrophobic and I start to get shaky and sweaty.

It's very common for people to feel like this in huge crowds.

My own father is also very intolerant of crowds! Funny enough, some people love it though, and being surrounded by crowds of people and noise is actually like a fix for them.

However, if you are like me and prefer the quieter life, then this is another one of my social anxiety tips that I have benefitted from a lot.

Choose to go out during off peak times, when public places are less busy.

I do my grocery shopping at 9pm at night or else early in the mornings, and it is such a pleasure!

Oh - and an added bonus tip here would be to avoid supermarkets at lunch hours at all costs!

Everyone is there buying lunch at these times!

Smile At Someone

This one works like a charm - if you can muster up the courage to do it!

Think about when someone smiles at you.

Don't you just instantly feel as though that person likes you because they took the time to smile at you? You feel a nice energy in the air and it makes you somehow feel at ease.

So now, it's your turn to smile at someone.

I realize when you have social anxiety that it can be hard to work up the courage to do it, but it will be SO worth it!

Just do it!

It will take you 3 seconds, and you can make someone's day just by taking the time to simply be nice, plus you will feel so good inside!

SIDE NOTE: *Did you know that it take 28 muscles to frown but only 17 to smile?*

Eating and Diet Reminders

Diet

One of the changes I had to make in my lifestyle was that of my diet.

We often brush off the importance of a healthy diet as something that is cliché, because we hear it from every single person and in every self-help book or website that we read.

The thing that I find is, people don't understand why they need to change their diets. We just think of certain foods as unhealthy or healthy for us, but do we really understand why they are healthy or unhealthy?

When I began to understand the biology and physiology of how the human body worked and the effect that everything I put in my mouth had on the body, it made a lot more sense to me, and suddenly those repetitive, "Eat a healthy diet" slogans began to actually get through to me!

Now, not only did I write an entire chapter on diet in my first book, 'My Anxiety Companion,' but I've also done videos on the importance of diet if you suffer with an anxiety disorder, and how certain foods can trigger or alleviate certain symptoms that come along with anxiety.

You can watch these videos on the YouTube channel entitled 'My Anxiety Companion'

Firstly, it is vitally important to eat a fresh and wholesome diet and to greatly limit refined foods and processed convenience foods. As far as I am concerned, the number one key word when focusing on a healthy diet is the word "wholefood" This means foods which are in their natural state or as close to their natural state as possible – foods that you can literally pick and eat.

We need to eat real foods, not processed man-made junk with about 20 strange and unpronounceable ingredients! There are so many different diet plans out there, and no matter what kind of diet you are following, I think we can all agree that a healthy diet to follow would be one rich in fresh fruit and vegetables, and these should be what most of your diet should consist of.

Of course, I'm not saying that we should never indulge and have a treat day – by all means, we all need to sometimes just kick back and have a junk food day, but the point is to keep these to occasional days.

If you can focus on eating fresh, nutrient dense, clean foods and try your best to make everything from scratch, instead of taking the more convenient way and purchasing a ready-made preservative laden meal, you will be fine.

If you are eating a poor diet, I strongly recommend that you start making changes, because sometimes you will find that certain foods may be the very thing that is triggering off some of your anxiety symptoms.

Refined Sugar is one of the culprits.

Some very common refined sugar foods include:

- Fizzy Drinks
- Chocolates
- Cookies
- Donuts
- Sweets and Candy
- Cake

I find I am absolutely fine if I have minimal amounts of sugar, and I do have fructose or maple syrup in my herbal tea, and even one or two cookies are fine for me, but if I indulge and go to town, then it can affect me.

I actually experience shakiness and I get all jittery. I sometimes will even cry, then I laugh, then I get angry. Of course, you shouldn't be surprised to hear this because this is what refined sugar does to a person.

So, let's discuss the ever important why - why do these foods do this to a person and why are they bad for someone with an anxiety disorder?

It's for two reasons:

Firstly, when food is refined or processed, this means that it is stripped of all its natural goodness, in other words, vital nutrients are removed and replaced with artificial additives and preservatives to make it taste good.

If you were to eat a donut, the body recognizes it as being refined, and the fats from that donut need to be assimilated, (made part of the body), and in order to do that, the body needs vitamin B, but because all the vitamins have been destroyed in the refining process of that donut, the body has to leach vitamin B from what is already in the body.

B vitamins just so happen to be our anti stress vitamins – they keep our nervous system healthy.

Secondly, refined sugar increases our blood sugar to abnormal levels, making us feel good temporarily with what is described as a sugar high. The pancreas then has to release large amounts of insulin in order to bring our blood sugar down again, and because we've been on such a sugar high, we feel it more because our levels come down as quickly as they went up, resulting in low mood, irritability and sluggishness.

So, what do you eat if you crave sugary foods?

You eat fruit, and I can already see a lot of people throwing their hands up in the air, but think of it this way, would you rather have something contribute to your anxiety or not?

I honestly swear by eating a piece of fruit if craving something sweet!

99% of the time, I won't even feel like that unhealthy sweet treat afterwards!

Nowadays, you can get many healthy fruit and nut bars which taste delicious and use fruit such as dates for sweetener. It is highly important though that you check all the ingredients to make sure that it contains only fruit and nuts and no added sugar or preservatives. I recommend checking out the health food stores for this.

While we're on the subject of fruit, I would highly recommend getting yourself a box of medjool dates. These are extremely sweet and have a similar texture to fudge. If you have a sweet tooth, I can guarantee that this will satisfy it.

Make sure they contain no added sugar or preservatives!

Another thing I recommend for a sweet tooth is to check out the many raw dessert recipes that are available. My husband and I once made a raw oreo cheesecake – it was so delicious and so sweet!

If you would like an in depth read about refined sugar and chemicals, please refer to my book 'My Anxiety Companion.' Another book which I strongly recommend is Mary-Ann Shearer's 'The Natural Way' This book is a fantastic read for anyone wanting to change their diet and lifestyle.

Within the next few points of this book, I will also be telling you which foods to load up on to alleviate your anxiety symptoms and which vitamins and minerals you need an abundance of.

So, watch for those tips!

Image credit: Pixabay/manfredrichter

Eat Breakfast

Again, I feel this is another one of those clichéd tips, because everyone has heard the 'eat breakfast' slogan being shouted from the rooftops, and everyone knows that they should be doing it. So, at the risk of sounding like a broken record – here it goes.

It is very important to eat breakfast, but more important for people with anxiety disorders to eat breakfast, because of the impact not eating in the morning will have on your blood glucose levels. Your body has been without food and drink for approximately 8-10 hours, depending on how long you sleep.

Your body has taken that opportunity, while you rest, to break everything down and digest every morsel of food that you had to eat that day. When you wake up in the morning, your body is expecting you to eat something nutritious to kick start it so that it can provide glucose to your cells.

Without sufficient glucose, your blood sugar levels drop and you get left with a big load of emotions ranging from dizziness and fatigue to irritability.

I personally enjoy eating fruit or oats in the morning.

Not only is fruit healthy, but it satisfies the sweet tooth without disrupting the blood glucose levels, and oats provide a lot of fibre. I enjoy blending my fruit into a smoothie or healthy milkshake or else I'll eat the oats with a chopped-up banana.

Herbal Tea Instead Of Caffeine

Coffee and Tea are very sore subjects for a lot of people.

There are some people who cannot function without their early morning cuppa, and let's face it, the corporate office would not be quite the same without the much-loved coffee machine.

It's perfectly natural to see why coffee and tea are comforting, they are warming and they help wake us up.

However, we all know by now that coffee and tea are not the best drinks to be ingesting.

When it comes to people who suffer with anxiety disorders, there is no exception, and you will be doing yourself a grand favour if you try to cut down, or better yet eliminate, these drinks from your diet.

Coffee and tea also leave very bad withdrawal symptoms such as irritability and headaches when trying to quit, and this is why so many people are unsuccessful when they try to cut down or stop completely.

There are two reasons why anxiety sufferers should not be drinking coffee and ordinary black tea:

Caffeine is a stimulant which sets off adrenaline, which will then cause similar flight or fight symptoms that we spoke about earlier. This includes increased heart rate and upsetting of the central nervous system. This is why it is used to keep people awake.

The tannins in tea act as a diuretic, meaning that it will cause you to urinate more than usual, which will result in dehydration. The effects of dehydration can range from headaches to anxiety to irritability.

I'm not saying it is an easy habit to kick, as I myself was once a coffee and tea addict, but now that strong smell inside a coffee shop is enough to make me feel sick to my stomach!

I gave up caffeine about 5 years ago, and I only drink herbal tea now, but even so, I'm still not a big tea drinker!

Decaffeinated coffee and tea may be a good alternative if you're really struggling to kick your caffeine habit, but bear in mind that decaf is not all it's cracked up to be. First of all, decaf drinks are not actually 100% caffeine free. Although about 97% of the caffeine has been removed, there is still between 3 and 18 milligrams of caffeine in a 12-ounce cup of decaf coffee, but it is a good place to start if you're really struggling.

Secondly, decaf drinks are very acidic which causes mineral loss such as magnesium and calcium.

I speak more about this in the points on vitamins and minerals, and why this affects anxiety sufferers.

Furthermore, if you're looking after your health, which you should be doing anyway, then decaf drinks have had most of their antioxidants removed during the extraction process, which does absolutely nothing for your health.

If you are one of those people who struggle to drink herbal tea, go to a health shop and buy a pack of readymade tea that has a few different herbs mixed together.

There are many varieties and many aimed at relaxation and sleep.

If you still really struggle to drink herbal tea, then add a bit of maple syrup to the tea, but don't add milk or creamer.

Image credit: Pixabay/Scym

Starch

Contrary to popular belief about not eating starchy foods at night, it could actually be a good thing to have something like a baked potato with your dinner.

This is because starchy foods have been shown to increase the serotonin production in the body. Serotonin is a feel-good hormone which converts to melatonin, and melatonin is responsible for making us feel sleepy.

Carbohydrates are very important in the diet because they are what fuel our cells.

Remember I spoke about fruit earlier and how wonderful it is for supplying good natural sugar to our cells? Well starchy complex carbohydrates do the same by also supplying us with much needed sugar for our cells.

Complex carbohydrates are slow releasing, making you feel fuller longer, and when the body has broken them down and converted them to glucose, your body will have the necessary fuel it needs.

I am by no means telling you to overdo it, but adding a low fat complex carbohydrate to one of your meals every other day will probably do you a lot of good and your body will not only thank you, but you'll get that serotonin boost!

Try it out - see if it makes a difference.

If I'm being honest here, I do find that I feel more satisfied and full when I eat a potato or some rice with dinner.

Image credit: Pixabay/RitaE

Anti-Stress Vitamins

There are two vitamins that are vital for anxiety sufferers.

Vitamin B complex, our anti stress vitamins, and then Vitamin D, without which our anti stress minerals cannot function properly!

Vitamin B complex – Found in a huge variety of foods, including green leafy vegetables, fruit, seeds, and whole grains with the exception of vitamin B12. This vitamin is actually a bacteria that is made in the soil, but because our soil is not what it once was due to pesticides and climate change, it may be best to get checked for vitamin B12 deficiency, as this vitamin in particular plays a huge part in maintaining a healthy nervous system.

For me personally, I take a vitamin B12 supplement in a spray form. Always make sure that you choose a supplement with methylcobalamin and not cyanocobalamin, which is a cheaper synthetic chemical and doesn't absorb as well as methylcobalamin.

Around 40% of people are vitamin B12 deficient even if you're eating a lot of red meat, so if you suspect you are running low, or if low B12 runs in your family – please get tested.

Vitamin D – It has been drummed into our heads that we must stay out of the sun and wear sunscreen every day. However, no living thing can actually survive and thrive without sunlight, and we as human beings are no different. You should be spending 20 minutes outdoors every other day, or every day if you can, in order to get your dose of sunshine so that your body can make vitamin D. This vitamin is important as calcium cannot absorb without it (I'll talk about calcium in the next tip.) Also getting a nice dose of natural light will aid in increasing your serotonin levels!

Anti-Stress Minerals

These are two anti-stress minerals that are vital for mental health:

Calcium – A deficiency in calcium may result in osteoporosis, but mentally, it will result in an inability to relax. Calcium is very easy to get hold of in abundance. I don't recommend eating dairy, so instead of dairy products these are my suggestions for good calcium sources: sesame seeds, dried figs, green leafy vegetables, broccoli, and most fruit, especially oranges.

Magnesium – Like calcium, magnesium helps us to relax and if you don't get enough then you could become nervous and irritable. Healthy sources for magnesium include green leafy vegetables, whole grains, seeds, apples, and beetroot.

SIDE NOTE: In my first book, 'My Anxiety Companion,' I dedicated an entire chapter to diet, vitamins, and minerals, and I explain everything in much more detail there. I also explain acidity and alkalinity and why I don't recommend dairy products as a reliable calcium source.

Alcohol

Here we have yet another thing that the whole world knows is bad for you, but ironically people use it as a form of relaxation and to escape their problems, so it's no wonder that people with mental illness tend to use not only smoking, but alcohol as well, as a means to escape their torment.

I gave up drinking 5 years ago - not that I was a big drinker in any case.

Occasionally I will have a sip of cider, as my husband likes to drink it, but otherwise I don't drink. Quite honestly, I don't enjoy it, and I never really understood the fetish for it. It makes me dehydrated, lethargic, and gives me a headache and a dry mouth.

After a night out with my girlfriends, I would always feel very jittery and my tongue had a strange taste – especially the next day.

Alcohol has different effects on people, and those who use it to forget their reality often start to abuse it, and unfortunately this makes mental illness worse because of pure dependency and addiction from the 'feel good' moments that alcohol provides.

Like smoking, alcohol affects the brain, and this will, in turn, affect your moods and emotions.

It also lowers your serotonin levels.

If you do drink, try these tips:

- Eat something substantial before you start drinking
- Drink a glass of water between every drink that you have to avoid dehydration. This will also help you to reduce the number of alcohol drinks you have, as the water will fill you up
- Try and mix your alcohol in other non-alcoholic beverages

SIDE NOTE: *Never drink alcohol alongside medication!*

Lifestyle Reminders

Eliminate Chemicals

Like most people, I had always heard of chemicals in our everyday food and house hold products, but I never really thought much of them.

It was only after I read Mary-Ann Shearer's book 'The Natural Way' that I really started to take notice of just how chemicals are making their way into every corner of our lives.

Not only that, but I was shocked when I read about the harmful effects that they can have on mental health!

I was always thinking that chemicals only caused physical side effects, but I never stopped to think about what the mental effects were!

We live in a day and age where convenience and technology seem to take a lead in everything, and our food and product supplies are no exception.

Supermarkets are full of pre-packaged food, full of additives with false claims of it being healthy.

These commercial products are loaded with chemicals and cheap harmful ingredients.

Let's have a look at a few common ingredients found in our everyday food and products.

I will also mention some of the mental effects that they can cause:

- Sodium benzoate and other benzoates – These preservatives are identified by the numbers E210–E219 and can be found in margarines, some sodas, and bottled condiments such as pickled products, jellies, and sauces. These can cause hyperactivity
- Calcium propionate – Identified by the number E282, this preservative is used in all sorts of breads and can contribute to migraines and behavioural changes
- Aspartame – Aspartame's E number is E951 and you may know it as Canderel, NutraSweet, or one of those other artificial sweeteners. It is said to be 200 times sweeter than sucrose. It also popular in diet sodas, and many times when something says 'sugar free' it could have aspartame in it, so always check the label! Aspartame is said to be

linked to anxiety, depression, irritability, insomnia, and behavioural changes, and nervous, endocrine, and hormonal system disorders
- Monosodium glutamate - (E621). This is commonly known as "MSG," and is used to enhance flavour by tricking our taste buds into believing that there is more flavour in the food than what there actually is.

MSG is very common in pre-packaged soups, bouillon cubes, and canned foods, and can cause headaches and chest pain. While these are physical conditions, headaches can lead to irritability and chest pains can lead to panic. If I happen to eat something with MSG in it, I get all jittery!

It's really quite alarming that these extremely harmful additives seem to be lurking in nearly all the products that we put into and onto our bodies!

That is why it is very important that you get into a habit of label reading and start eliminating these harsh chemicals from your lifestyle and environment.

If you just start to spend a little more time and research a bit, you will nearly always find another brand of the same product that focuses on a more natural approach.

This applies to not only our food choices, but our beauty and body products and household cleaners.

Obviously, we cannot get away from chemicals completely, but even just eliminating some basic products and replacing them with non-chemical brands will benefit not only your physical but your mental well-being as well.

Be Careful Of What You Read and Watch On TV

I have been married for nearly 10 years and in those years of being married, my husband and I have not once watched a news broadcast, and for that matter, we have never bought or read a newspaper. This is because the stories that appear on the news or in newspapers are mostly filled with negativity and political stuff that frankly you don't need in your life.

You are not shutting yourself out from the world, you are protecting yourself. If something is that important that it will actually affect you, trust me, you'll find out about it somewhere and somehow.

This leads me to my next point: movies that are of a violent and graphic nature.

Please don't watch movies like this. They are so psychologically damaging, and nowadays, movies don't hold anything back. It seems the more blood, gore and horror, the more people like them, which is truly astounding in my opinion.

Before I got struck down with anxiety disorder, I loved to watch the scariest horrors I could find, and movies that messed with my mind were the best, but not anymore. I simply cannot expose myself to things like that anymore because it traumatizes me.

So please when selecting what to watch on TV, opt for light hearted and funny movies instead. If you enjoy a bit of a thriller, then there are plenty of light hearted mystery movies to watch instead of violent and anxiety provoking ones!

Don't Watch Medical TV Programmes

Another thing that I've had to change within my lifestyle is no longer watching medical TV shows.

I feel this is a very important tip to live by because when our anxiety is at its peak, we become irrational and start to overreact. I used to love watching programmes where people got mysterious illnesses and documentaries with people who had rare diseases, but I simply cannot do it anymore.

I found that if I watched a medical show on TV, I would actually start to imagine the same thing happening to me, and it sent me into anxiety overdrive. You literally make yourself believe that you have the same medical condition as the person you saw on TV, and the mind is so powerful that you start displaying symptoms of the illness. It's not something that you can even help, it just happens. I also found that the rarer the disease and the more distressing, the more anxious it made me.

Honestly guys, you don't need this added stress of knowing about all the weird and rare illnesses that could creep up on you! Just don't watch shows like this. I would also recommend not reading stories in magazines about people who have strange and rare illnesses. If you happen to stumble across a story like this in a magazine – just page past it!

Now I want to tell you what happened to me.

I didn't watch a medical programme, but my grandfather was seriously ill at the same time that my anxiety was at one of its bad stages, and one of the symptoms he had terrified me so much that I convinced myself that I had it as well.

To this day, it still was one of my most distressing symptoms and as horrible as it sounds, it may be a good idea to limit your time around sick friends and family members as well. This doesn't mean avoid them completely, just reduce how much time you spend around them.

It's not that you don't care – it's just, unfortunately, a necessary thing that you have to do – for peace of mind.

Smoking

Despite what people say about smoking to relieve their stress, cigarette smoke actually induces anxiety.

People who suffer from mental disorders tend to smoke more, and because the nicotine in the cigarette is so addictive, the body naturally wants more and more, just like coffee.

The smoker will feel relaxed for a short time as the nicotine reaches the brain, but after a short while, the nicotine starts to cause changes within the brain, and the withdrawal symptoms start to kick in, which result in another cigarette being lit up.

Another thing to bear in mind is that because of the changes in the brain, hormone disruption is very common as well.

It ends up being a constant cycle of dependence, addictiveness, and withdrawal symptoms. The withdrawal symptoms are similar to that of coffee: anxiety, depression, irritability, headaches etc.

Keep Your Surroundings Clean

I feel that with regard to anxiety, keeping a tidy house is not emphasized enough, and I feel that it does make a difference.

There's a saying that goes, "A tidy house is a tidy mind," and it rings true for me.

Growing up I was an exceptionally untidy person and used to make my Mom so frustrated because I just couldn't keep things neat and tidy.

Now being a wife and having my own house to keep clean, I appreciate keeping my surroundings tidy and I actually find it does help my mental health as well.

As I've grown older, I am finding just how much dirtiness and untidiness can make me feel instantly anxious.

It really is incredible!

I never used to be like this, but somehow when everything has its place, I feel relaxed.

Image credit: Pixabay/Stevepb

Get A Pet

Studies have actually shown that animals can be great companions for people who suffer with mental illness.

Animals are truly incredible creatures and I am actually a huge animal lover myself!

They give so much and ask so little in return. They give unconditional love, loyalty, and never ever judge us. Some animals actually get trained up as therapy pets and go around to different hospitals and homes to comfort sick and elderly people.

My two dogs are not registered therapy pets, but they are so amazing and they always seem to know when I am sad.

When I'm feeling down in the dumps, I love nothing better than to hug my dogs and feel their soft fur against me. They just offer such calming energy.

If you don't have a pet, perhaps consider getting one, I promise you they are truly a gift.

SIDE NOTE: *If you are going to consider getting yourself a pet, please go to a rescue shelter and adopt an animal in need of a home. Shelters have the most beautiful animals in all shapes, sizes and ages. Both my dogs are rescues and they seem to know they were given a second chance* ☺

The little fur ball in the photo below is one of my beautiful rescue babies!

Image credit: Author's own

Spring Clean

It still astounds me how therapeutic this can be.

This is one of the greatest tips that I know of to practice letting go.

Letting go of physical things can be hard, but letting go of stuck emotions such as resentment, jealousy and anger is even more difficult.

As we throw stuff out that we no longer need, we practice letting go.

Donating unwanted items gives us that warm feeling of helping others.

The act of donating and letting go of physical items creates a ripple effect to help us let go of emotional baggage as well.

Force Your Hobbies

Having a hobby means that we enjoy doing something that interests us and makes us happy. We enjoy spending time throwing all our energy and passion into it.

Why is this?

It's because it makes us happy and relaxed.

Doing things we enjoy is also very therapeutic. Everyone has different things that interest them, so everyone will have a different hobby, and what interests me may be dead boring to you and vice versa.

However, it is not uncommon for anxiety sufferers to actually lose complete interest in their hobbies when they are going through a rough time with their anxiety. This is actually the time when you need your hobbies the most and it can be a good idea to literally force yourself to take up your hobby again, or else to ask a trusted friend or family member to help force you to try do your hobby. I spoke about this in my last book, but I'll give another short example.

Let's say that you are passionate about painting and were taking weekly classes, but your anxiety or depression has literally made you lose any interest that you had in it. This is when you need to ask a family member or friend that you trust to help force you to get in the car and go to the class to paint. They could even drive you to the class and sit with you while you paint. Yes – it is that important to do this, and I stress to friends and family members to please play your part seriously.

However, the all-important question is this: How do we force ourselves to do something that we have no desire to do?

That is why it is so important to have a very trusted family member or friend to literally pick you up off the couch and put you in the situation so that you are forced to do it. What if you have no one to help you? Then you have to force yourself and it is absolutely incredible how creative you can become in order to force yourself to do something. We all have had those conversations with people who say in mid-sentence, "Yes, and I had to actually force myself to do that." We've all heard that sentence and we've all said it to someone else as well.

Why do you think people force themselves to do things?

It's for the pure and simple reason that they have to.

You hear your alarm clock telling you to get up, and you force yourself out of bed, because you know that if you don't, you won't get to work on time, which could mean that you will lose your job, which means you will have no income, which means no food and no roof over your head.

When we have to force ourselves to do something, it often helps to think of the "what if" scenario. Now obviously this is a bit different because we are applying this to our hobbies, happy things, and not something serious like getting up to go to work. So, we have to approach it a bit differently.

So, let's use the painting example again. What will happen if you don't get up out of bed and go and paint? Well, maybe you could tell yourself that if you lie around the whole day, you won't sleep that night, because you've been lying about and sleeping during the day.

Perhaps you need to paint because if you don't, your paints will start to dry up and you would have wasted your money.

Perhaps someone actually asked you to paint them something and you've been procrastinating. You could also place happy things around the space where you paint to make it more inviting. Put on some music, have a cup of tea, post happy pictures around the room, put some fresh flowers in your painting space to encourage you to go work. I promise you that changing your space to a happier and brighter one can really influence your mood. I used to have this colour changing candle along with a small indoor water feature. I literally loved going to work on my computer because I knew that I could listen to the sound of the water and watch the candle changing colours.

How often do people grab a nice cup of tea and put relaxing music on when they have to do something they're forced to do? This is because it helps to make the task more likable and manageable.

As you can see, it is a tough one, but one that is quite necessary and one that can work well. You could also try breaking it up into smaller bits. So, tell yourself you will dedicate 30 minutes to painting every day, and not the usual 3 hours that you would usually spend. Also, maybe you could reward yourself, and I would normally recommend a tasty treat, but because refined foods and sugar are not good for us anxiety sufferers, you are going to reward yourself in other ways.

First of all, you are going to decide how many 'forces' you want to do.

So, let's say you decide that for every five times that you forced yourself to spend thirty minutes painting every day, that you can go and buy those new shoes you've been eyeing.

Do you see how this is going to work?

SIDE NOTE 1: *Just in case you are wondering – my husband used to force me to play Nintendo wii games with him, and my mother used to force me to do all sorts of activities as well, just to take my mind off the anxiety. Most of the time – it really helped!*

SIDE NOTE 2: *Please use common sense here. Obviously when I talk about forcing your hobbies, I mean basic hobbies like painting, photography, gardening, or cooking, etc. If you have social anxiety, then obviously going to a busy outdoor event is not going to do you much good, so when I talk about forcing your hobbies - I mean within reason! Oh, and also hobbies that include things like substance abuse are completely excluded from this!*

Natural Medicine Suggestions

St John's Wort

St John's Wort is a very popular natural herbal remedy that can be taken in place of medication.

It is used for stress relief, anxiety, depression and insomnia. Unlike rescue remedy though, St John's Wort should not be taken alongside conventional medicine.

Although it is a natural remedy, and a wonderful alternative for people who cannot or don't wish to take conventional medication, it is important to remember that there can be side effects and you must always check with a doctor before you take, reduce, or change anything when it comes to medicine, whether herbal or conventional.

Rescue Remedy

Rescue remedy is one of my absolute favourite natural remedies.

First of all, it can be taken alongside conventional medication. Secondly it comes in drop form, pill form, and spray form.

Personally, I prefer the tablet form, I just find it works better for me, and there are different brands, with the one from Dr Bach being one of the more common ones.

Rescue remedy is made up of 5 different flower essences, and 3-5 drops on the tongue can be taken 3 times a day or else 2-3 of the tablets when very anxious or stressed out.

I have been using rescue remedy for years and I have not had a problem or any side effects, however please check with your doctor or with a health professional before taking any herbal remedy, especially if you're taking any other medication.

Bach Flower Remedies

The Bach Flower remedies were founded by Dr Edward Bach and consist of 38 flower essences.

The Bach system is built on the belief that each remedy is linked to an emotion.

Each remedy comes from a different flower and is mixed in brandy and stored in a 30ml glass bottle. They also come with a dropper for easy usage.

The remedies can be taken neat or diluted in a bit of water, and you can actually mix and match remedies together, depending on what 'emotion' you are treating.

Although there are 38 remedies in total, they have been divided into 7 groups with each group being for a different emotion.

It is important to note that the Bach system doesn't treat physical ailments.

Instead they focus on treating the emotional effects caused by the ailment and help to alleviate the negativity and worsening of the ailment being experienced.

The Dr Bach rescue remedy is known as the crisis formula. This consists of 5 different flower essences that are mixed in one bottle.

SIDE NOTE 1: Although the Bach remedies are said to be safe to use when pregnant, I still recommend consulting a health professional.

SIDE NOTE 2: Although it is unlikely that there would be any problems with taking the flower remedies alongside other medication, I would recommend consulting with a doctor before taking any herbal remedies. From a personal point of view, I took

Bach remedies with my other medication, and I didn't have any problems when I used them.

SIDE NOTE 3: The remedies are preserved in brandy. If you are avoiding alcohol for whatever reason, you have to first speak to your doctor before taking the remedies.

Breathing Exercises

Blow Up A Balloon

This is another very strange hack, but it makes a lot of sense when you think about it.

This technique works because it forces us to breathe deeply instead of shallowly like so many of us do.

When we blow up a balloon, we usually inhale slowly and deeply, and then blow out deeply and for as long as we can into the balloon to make it inflate.

When we are anxious or especially when we are having a panic attack, our breathing becomes short and shallow, causing hyperventilation.

The breathing required to blow up a balloon is the exact opposite.

The 4-4-4-4 breath

I just call this breathing technique the 4-4-4-4 breath because I don't know what else to call it ☺

This breath is fabulous to do if you start feeling panicky.

The reason is because you are counting to 4 for every inhale and exhale and you are holding for 4 counts in between every inhale and exhale that you take.

This counting and holding technique is what prevents hyperventilation.

You don't specifically have to use 4 counts. You can actually inhale and exhale for a shorter or longer amount of time.

If you prefer to do a 2-4-2-4 breathing sequence, that is absolutely fine.

To do this breathing technique:

- Get comfortable. You can stand, sit, lie down, keep your eyes open or keep them closed. You can listen to music or have silence. It's up to you.

- Breathe normally for a few breaths to just get relaxed and comfortable for the breathing exercise to come.
- Inhale for 4 counts (or however many counts you wish to use), hold your breath for 4 counts, exhale for 4 counts and then hold for another 4 counts before starting the sequence again.
- You can repeat this exercise as many times as you wish.

SIDE NOTE: If you start to feel dizzy, just resume normal breathing. The dizziness is caused by the body not being used to breathing in so fully and deeply. If this happens to you, it is best to build up this type of breathing slowly.

The Candle Breath

This is a breathing technique that helps you to focus as well because you are deep breathing and you are focusing on the flame of a candle.

The object is to place a small candle in front of you, leave about 30-40cm in between you and the candle, inhale deeply and then blow out onto the candle flame just so it flickers but doesn't blow out completely.

It will help you to breathe more steadily and, because you're focusing on not blowing out the candle, it helps to take your mind off the anxiety. You will see how focusing on not blowing the flame out helps to control your breath on exhaling.

Focusing on the flame also has an incredibly soothing effect.

Image credit: Pixabay/monicore

To do this breathing technique:

- Get a small table or box that meets your chin level.
- Place a small candle on the table and sit comfortably in front of the table about 30-40cm away from the candle.
- Light the candle and inhale for 3-4 counts (or however many counts you wish) and then exhale for 3-4 counts and

repeat until you feel calm. Focus on not blowing out the candle.

SIDE NOTE: *If you suffer from epilepsy, the flicker of the candle may bother you or trigger an attack, so please if you are in doubt, check with a doctor or else refrain from doing this particular breath.*

The Five Senses Breath

I love this technique so much!

I use it during my meditation, I use it to help me get to sleep, when I'm stressed, and especially when I feel panicky!

You may have seen or heard something similar whereby if you feel a panic attack coming on, look around and find 5 things you can see, 4 things you can touch, 3 things you can hear, 2 things you can smell and 1 thing you can taste.

This works very well and I have used it before.

However, I decided to try something a bit different also using the five senses, and I'm now addicted.

So first of all, sit or lie down.

Close your eyes and breathe in deeply through the nose and out through your mouth.

Do this five times, but each time, you are going to envision a different sense for the air you are breathing in, and because your eyes will be closed, you will have to use imagery and a lot of concentration to 'envision' your five senses!

- Breathe in and see what the air looks like. I usually envision white light going into my nose. When you breathe out, imagine smoke coming out your mouth.
- Next, breathe in and feel what your breath feels like. Does it feel cool against your nostrils? Breathe out and feel the warmth of your breath coming out your mouth.
- Then breathe in again and hear your breath. Then hear your breath as you exhale out your mouth.
- Breathe in again, and smell the air going into your nose. Smell it going out your nose when you exhale. Perhaps you want to imagine it smelling like a rose.
- Breathe in once more and taste the air. Maybe you want to envision a sweetness when you breathe in and a sour taste when you breathe out.

You are welcome to repeat this as many times as you like.

Please give it a try - this breathing technique is a winner!

Relaxation Hacks

Meditation

Personally, meditation has helped me a lot.

I have a very active and wild imagination, and meditation has helped me to calm my mind and to focus on the moment. It is also a wonderful self-care technique, because it teaches you to focus on taking quiet time for yourself, and to not feel guilty about taking out that time.

Another thing I love about meditation is that it gives me those few special minutes to just escape this world, and completely immerse myself in total relaxation.

Meditation can take a bit of getting used to, but it really helps to relax the mind and body, and I really can recommend it for anxiety sufferers.

Meditation, literally is when a person tries to clear the mind – just totally free it of any clutter and chaos, until it becomes totally still. It's not easy, especially for us anxiety sufferers whose minds are constantly chattering away to us, however the mental chatter is quite normal and you will always hear in guided meditations,

"Just focus on the breath," which helps you to stop paying attention to the thoughts.

Meditation can be done sitting or lying down, with or without music and with open eyes or closed eyes. Some meditations are guided, whereby a person takes you through the meditation by using imagery, and some meditations just play music and you can do your own meditation. Some meditations can also be done using visual anchors such as mandalas and candles. Meditation lengths vary, and some can be as short as five minutes or as long as two hours.

If you have never done meditation before, I suggest using a meditation for beginners and just do five minutes until you are comfortable with it and then gradually build it up.

You can get hold of meditations very easily.

I find YouTube very handy because there are so many different meditations on there. I personally prefer a guided meditation and I'll listen to a bit first to see whose voice I can connect with, and if I like the meditation imagery.

You can also get meditation apps that you can buy, or else you can buy them from meditation websites or on a good old-fashioned CD at new age shops.

Image credit: Pixabay/leninscape

Aromatherapy

Another clichéd tip, I know, but I love it and it has really helped me, and thousands of other people out there ☺

If I ever have a medical issue, the first thing I am inclined to do is to go read up on aromatherapy remedies first.

Aromatherapy can treat a wide variety of different ailments including both physical and mental.

As I am quite sure that you all know what aromatherapy is, I will keep the explanation very short and focus more on some of my favourite aromatherapy recipes ☺

Aromatherapy is when the oil from plants is extracted and used for physical and mental healing. When we refer to essential oils, we are referring to neat oils, which have not been diluted in carrier oil, such as grape seed oil.

In order to use aromatherapy oils safely on the skin, they need to be diluted first. The general guideline is usually 10 drops of essential oil to 30ml of carrier oil.

Image credit: Pixabay/monicore

Some of my favourite aromatherapy oils include:

Ylang Ylang – This is my favourite scent of all the oils. It is divine to smell. A recipe that I love is 5 drops of Ylang Ylang and 5 drops of Lavender. Put this in your bath or else use it as a massage blend. Just remember to mix the neat oils with a carrier oil such as grape seed before using it directly on the skin.

Chamomile – This is a very gentle and relaxing scent. I also enjoy drinking chamomile tea before bed. Please make sure that you purchase actual chamomile tea bags if you want to drink it!!!!

Lavender – What can lavender not do? It is so versatile and such a multipurpose oil. It is great for relaxation. I love putting a few drops in a bath or a diffuser, or else hang some fresh lavender flowers in an old stocking above your bed. It is also fantastic for tension headaches brought on by stress and anxiety.

A great technique for tension headaches is listed below from Margie Hare, an aromatherapist practicing in Australia:

- Use 1 drop of pure lavender oil in 1 ml of carrier oil such as grape seed oil or olive oil.
- Then find your pulse point on your temple and put pressure on the point. Massage the oil 3 times clockwise and then 3 times counter clockwise, then put pressure on the point again.
- Then move down to your neck, find the pulse point, and apply the same technique.

- Then move to your armpit, find the pulse, and apply the same technique, and finally find your pulse on your wrist and do the same technique.
- Do this twice.
- Afterward, lie in a dark room for at least 30 minutes with a cold washcloth across your forehead, rinsed in lavender oil.
- Make sure the windows in the room are open wide.

SIDE NOTE 1: *Always make sure that you blend your chosen oil in a carrier oil. This could be grape seed oil, jojoba oil, sweet almond oil (those with nut allergies beware), or even olive oil. This is because essential (neat) oils are extremely potent and may irritate the skin. You only need to blend the oils if you are using them on your skin. If you are using them in a bath or vaporizer, there is no need to blend them. Most oils are available at pharmacies and health stores.*

SIDE NOTE 2: *While aromatherapy is a safe and natural alternative, some oils are not suitable for people with certain conditions.*

SIDE NOTE 3: *Please always check for contraindications, and check with a doctor or aromatherapist if you are on medication or are* pregnant, epileptic, or have high blood pressure, or if you are otherwise unsure about something.

SIDE NOTE 4: Please seek advice before using aromatherapy oils, especially if you have never used them before.

Balloon Stress Ball

Have you ever noticed when people are stressed that they clench their fists, it's a common quirk of anxious people – myself included. This is where this tip comes in very handy.

Get a balloon and put some flour, powder or sugar into it and when you get stressed, squeeze it with all your might.

If you're not in the mood for DIY, then go to a toy store and purchase a soft ball that you can squeeze, or, if you're feeling strong, squeeze a tennis ball!

Keep a few of these around where you will be bound to pick them up.

A good place to keep one is by your computer or work space.

Ground Yourself / Mindfulness

Mindfulness seems to be the word on everyone's lips of late. Everyone wants to know how to do it, and it's actually really simple.

To be mindful means to focus on the present moment and to be open to whatever thoughts or feelings come your way.

This enables us to accept the challenges that we experience. When we are not grounded, we feel foggy or hazy in the head, and we don't really feel like ourselves.

I like this technique when I experience brain fog or when everything just becomes too much in my mind.

By grounding ourselves, we bring ourselves back to the present moment.

Here are some tips to help ground yourself:

- Just let whatever thoughts come to you come and pass. This applies to both the good and the bad thoughts. Don't try to push any of them away, just accept whatever comes your way.

- Practice deep breathing. Breathe in through your nose for a count of 4 and then exhale for a count of 5. By doing this, you will relax the body and soon the anxious thoughts will pass.
- Try and keep your feet directly on the ground. This is a great tip for when you're feeling very stressed and you need to ground yourself quickly. Close your eyes and plant your feet firmly on the ground and imagine a connection to the earth while deep breathing. This is even better if you can do it on grass or soil.
- If you are unable to close your eyes and you are in a public place, then this technique is awesome! Take note of your surroundings and focus on things you can see, feel, hear, smell, and taste. Focusing on colours helps as well.

Massage and Pull Your Ears

Say what??

Yes, you did read that correctly. When you feel stressed, try gently massaging your ears, especially the lobes, and pulling on them very gently. It is surprisingly very calming and a very nice feeling – especially if someone else does this!

When I used to do Indian head massages, I always included an ear massage, and everyone would comment on it.

The ears have many pressure points which, when stimulated, affect the whole body.

Feel good endorphins are released by the brain when the ears are touched, massaged or pulled.

SIDE NOTE: *Just a little fun fact – If you've ever watched the movie 'Rush Hour' you'll see that the Captain massages his ears to relieve his stress!*

Blow Cool Air Onto Your Thumb

You probably think that I've completely lost the plot with this one but this is one of the weirdest calming hacks I've seen and done in a while!

When you feel stressed or anxious, try blowing cool air onto your thumb. It is said to be an instant calming aid!

The theory behind this is that it stimulates the vagus nerve, which will activate the parasympathetic nervous system!

I talk and explain more about the parasympathetic nervous system later on in this book ☺

What I actually do, when I'm sitting at my desk, is I combine this technique with deep breathing. So, I inhale deeply, and then as I exhale, I blow the cool air onto my thumb.

I do it about five times.

Get A Desktop Zen Garden

I love a Zen Garden, whether they are big and in the yard, or whether they are small and on a table.

These originate from Japan and represent the dry landscapes of Japanese Zen Buddhism.

The idea is to recreate a landscape by using rocks and making swirls (which represent water) in the sand with a small rake.

You can also add other props such as statues, plants, or butterflies. Everyone's garden will be different, there is no 'one' way to do this.

Zen gardens provide:

- It is very relaxing and meditative.
- Creating the swirls and placing the props brings about your creative side and brings out the inner child.
- You bring nature right to your desk.

Image credit: Pixabay/marcovincenti

Himalayan Salt Lamps

Oh, my word – I just love my salt lamp - well technically speaking, mine is actually a candle lamp, but it still does the trick!

It mesmerizes me every time I look at it because it's so pretty, but salt lamps can actually play a really awesome role in your home!

Everything on earth is made of energy, including human beings, and within that energy, positive and negative ions are constantly being produced by each and every thing around us.

Positive ions come from electronic things like cell phones and computers, whereas something like a plant produces negative ions. This explains why nature is so calming because plants are releasing all those negative ions into the air, whereas positive ions actually cause chemical imbalances in the brain.

It's also interesting to note that in this day and age of technology and computers, anxiety and stress are the highest they've ever been.

Now that you have received your science lesson, let's look at why these lamps are so good for anxiety:

- They counteract positive ions! The bigger the lamp, the more negative ions it will emit, dispelling the positive ions from your surroundings.
- The rock that the lamp is made of has up to 84 trace minerals which the body can absorb, resulting in a healthier you.

- Negative ions give you energy by improving oxygen flow to the brain.

Image credit: Author's own

Popping Plastic

I honestly don't know what it is about popping the bubbles on popping plastic that is so therapeutic.

I can sit while watching a movie and just pop away – to the great annoyance of my husband! So best do this when you are on your own.

Save every bit of bubble wrap that you can and store it in a box for when you have the urge to pop those bubbles! ☺

Reflex Points

You have probably all heard of the term 'reflexology' and it is quite an amazing therapy.

I actually have trained in this myself and have given it to quite a few people, and it is amazing what you can pick up about a person just by looking at their feet.

Reflexology is where certain points on the hands and feet are linked to organs and systems within the body, and when pressure is gently applied to them, it can help the body to bring about healing within that area.

It is said that if a certain pressure point is painful, then there is a blockage in that area, which could be resulting in unpleasant symptoms.

To give a few examples, if you suffer from a lot of headaches, the big toe area would be one of the points to work on.

Sometimes an area is painful when pressed on.

Say for example your digestive area is painful, it could indicate that your digestion is not working at its best. For us girls, during our period, or when we ovulate, the uterus area in our feet can become extremely painful.

Reflexology can be done on the hands or feet, but the feet are a more popular choice because the hands have become more desensitized as we use them more regularly than the feet.

So, taking into consideration all of the above, there are also reflex points that you can press for stress relief without having to go through a complete reflexology session.

Here are a few of them:

Solar plexus point – On your foot, directly under the ball of the foot and in line with the third toe, breathe in, and as you breathe out press gently with your thumb on that area. Do this three times. If someone can do it for you, it can be done on each foot at the same time.

Solar plexus hand point – You can work the same point on your hands by pressing on the middle of your palm. This point will be in line with the third finger and in line with the top of the thumb extension.

Big toe – This is a good place to massage because not only will it help alleviate tension headaches, but your Pituitary gland which is the boss 'so to speak' of the endocrine system (hormones) is located directly in the middle of the big toe. Directly under the big toe, where the toe joins onto the rest of the foot can always be massaged as this is the neck area, which holds a lot of stress.

SIDE NOTE 1: *Please note that as with all alternative healing practices, there are contra-indications such as pregnancy and high blood pressure. Please always check with a doctor if you have any medical issues or are taking medication.*

SIDE NOTE 2: *Please use a qualified and reputable reflexologist for all your reflexology sessions. If you prefer a whole-body treatment as opposed to just the feet or hands, then please get in touch with a qualified acupressure practitioner.*

The Naam Yoga Hand Trick

This is a really cool Eastern medicine trick that you can do practically anywhere and at any time!

Simply press the index finger of your dominant hand onto the soft indentation between the second and third knuckle of your other hand's index finger. There is apparently a nerve there that will loosen the area around your heart!

This is such an easy trick to do right at your desk, in front of the computer.

Colour Therapy

Colour therapy is a holistic form of therapy where colour is used to enhance the moods and emotions of people.

Colour is white light on different wavelengths that produce different colours depending where simple light reflects and refracts.

There are 7 main colours on the spectrum, with each having its own vibration and energy.

The 7 colours also relate to the energy centres known as chakras within our own bodies. For those who are not aware, our chakras run right down the centre of our bodies, and a blocked chakra is believed to cause physical or mental discomfort in that area.

By doing a chakra meditation or using crystals, you can help to restore the good energy.

I will list these below so it makes a bit more sense.

The chakras include:

- Base chakra – Red - Just above the pubic bone
- Sacral chakra – Orange – Just between the base chakra and below the diaphragm
- Solar plexus – Yellow – Just below the bottom of the rib cage
- Heart chakra – Pink/Green – Chest area
- Throat chakra – Blue – Throat area
- Third Eye chakra – Violet/Indigo – Between your eyes
- Crown chakra – White – Top of your head in the centre

Hopefully that makes a bit more sense?

Let's talk a bit about colour, because how you paint and decorate your surroundings can have an effect on your emotions. Even the clothes you wear can affect your mood for that day.

Think of a bedroom painted and decorated in red – this would ignite feelings of love and passion, whereas a child's nursery school may be painted in bright bold colours to express happiness, energy, and playfulness.

Seasonal Affective Disorder relates to this as well because during the winter months, some people can go into a depressive state because of the lack of light during this time, resulting in some sufferers having to buy a light box.

Let's now look at some colours you can make use of for stress relief:

- Nature colours work well. Pale blues can remind us of the sky and pale greens can remind us of plant life and grass. They're very calming colours and a lot of beauty salons make use of colours such as these.
- Orange colours are said to help with depression, and it also symbolizes the sun.
- Purple colours are well known to help with anxiety. Lavender and lilac colours are very popular for relieving stress.

As mentioned before, you could even wear something of colour to help you during the day.

Say for example, you have a speech that you need to say at work. You could wear a crystal necklace of blue colour, as the colour blue relates to the throat chakra (where the voice box is) to aid you in 'speaking up' clearly and with confidence.

Colouring in for adults as I mentioned before, is also a very popular form of colour therapy for the pure and simple reason that it uses colour to colour in the pictures, and colour automatically enhances our mood.

Image credit: Pixabay/kirtlane

The 5-Minute Rule

The 5-minute rule is challenging, which is why I only apply it for 5 minutes at a time.

It is a great technique to use when you have lots to think about and lots of mental chatter going through your mind.

When we are stressed or busy or just have lots of different thoughts on our minds, it is tough to relax, and even more tough to have some quiet time for ourselves, because that mental chatter just keeps finding a way to break through and back into our minds.

The 5-minute rule is when you are going to sit and try to completely not think of any of your stress for 5 minutes. Ask yourself if you can dedicate just 5 minutes to give your body and mind a break from everything that is going on in your mind. You can do this – it is 5 minutes – that is nothing!

You will sit yourself down, get comfortable, close your eyes, and just breathe how you want to breathe. If you want to breathe deeply, then do so. If you want to just breathe normally, then do so. You want to just breathe, and not count your inhales and exhales, focus on just inhaling or exhaling. Listening to the sounds you make as you inhale and exhale will help.

Whenever you start to think of what you need to do, say in your mind "5 minutes" and that will instantly remind you as to what and why you are doing what you are doing.

Work the mental chatter out of your mind by just focusing on your breath and remembering that it's just 5 minutes out of your day that you don't want to think about anything.

Autonomous Sensory Meridian Response (ASMR)

This technique gained a lot of popularity last year and since then it has been used as a valuable tool in helping people with all sorts of problems such as stress, anxiety, depression and insomnia.

ASMR is when a person experiences a tickle or shiver or prickly sensation on parts of their body, commonly the spine, neck, head and arms.

This sensation is brought on by various psychological and/or physical sensations that result in highly relaxing, euphoric, and happy feelings.

The two downsides of ASMR are: firstly, it is not scientifically proven so there is not much research on it, and secondly, and very sadly, not everyone has the ability to experience ASMR.

Some examples of ASMR include:

- Running water
- Having your hair played with
- Rustling of a biscuit packet
- Hearing food being cooked

- Tapping
- Softly whispering
- Making and/or playing with slime

Please don't despair if you have not yet experienced ASMR.

Simply listen to one of the many ASMR videos on YouTube and within time, you'll get to know what sparks your ASMR!

Here is a blog post that I wrote a while back on ASMR with a few links that you can check out as well:

http://www.myanxietycompanion.com/blog/what-is-asmr-here-are-11-examples-and-why-it-helps-anxiety

Fractal Therapy

A fractal is a repeated pattern that is either identical or similar to one another.

Most fractals can be found in nature, such as leaves, flowers, snowflakes, and clouds, but even staring at a picture of something like a mandala or something with swirls in it is enough to bring about the desired effect.

Staring at fractals has been shown to relieve stress in people by up to 60%.

Image credit: Pixabay/Wow_Pho

Psychology Methods and Therapies

Say Your Irrational Fears Out Loud

Sometimes when we hear something spoken out loud it does something to the brain which makes it more real and believable. However, in this particular instance, if you say your irrational fears out loud, you will actually start to see just how ridiculous they are. It also seems that the more you dramatize it, the more this technique works. I remember one time telling my husband about something that I was scared of, and when I finished telling him, we actually both starting giggling because it was so silly because the possibility of this fear coming true was slim to none.

To show an example, see below:

"I am afraid to drive to the shopping centre because I may have a car accident, and then I will injure myself, become paralysed, become a burden to my family, then they'll abandon me and I will die alone"

If the above example put a smile on your face or made you giggle a bit, then you are on the right track because you can agree then that the above scenario is totally irrational and is really not likely to happen, and even if a car accident were to happen, it is unlikely that you would become paralysed, and that your family would neglect you!

The thing is though, irrational fears are really what anxiety disorders are all about.

It's about fearing something that will most likely never happen to us, and I think this is because anxiety sufferers often don't know what they are fearing. We almost fear 'fear' or the unknown, and it is because of the unknown fears that these irrational fears come to light – at least that's what I think – hope that makes sense! ☺

SIDE NOTE: *The more ridiculous you make your irrational fear sound, the more the brain – and you, will see how silly it is!* ☺

Be Your Own Psychologist

It has taken most of my life to realize that talking to oneself is not crazy or delusional. It is actually just the opposite.

Talking to yourself makes you concentrate better, makes you wiser, and can help in problem solving.

It is also motivating and reassuring.

One thing that I love about talking to myself is that I can ask myself questions and always get the answers that I want to hear! ☺

Don't let anyone fool you – we all talk to ourselves sometimes!

Even while I am typing this book out, I am talking out loud about what to write down and asking myself questions about what I should include and what I should take out.

This is where this next technique comes into play.

This is a truly remarkable technique and I promise you it has worked well for me.

This involves a bit of role playing.

You will play the part of both the anxiety sufferer and the psychologist. The beauty is that it can be done silently, in your own mind or, if you are alone, you can talk out loud.

You can even talk to your dog or cat. It can be a few minutes long, or an hour—as long as you like.

You can cry, laugh, or make notes. There is no wrong or right way to do it. But the best thing of all is that you don't even have to believe your psychologist self.

The idea is to act like you are sitting in a psychologist's office, telling him or her about your anxiety. After you are done, you then take on the role of the psychologist. You will be amazed at what you tell your "anxiety" self, but you will be even more amazed at how you actually, deep down, already know the answers to your questions.

This technique is also great for recognizing and halting irrationality.

Check out the dialogue below to see how this can be done.

This scenario was actually something similar that happened to me when I needed to go to get some groceries and my social phobia started to play up:

Anxiety sufferer: I don't want to go to the shop because I am afraid of the other people who will be there.

Psychologist: Why are you afraid of people?

Anxiety sufferer: I just don't like the fact that they are strangers and that they look at me.

Psychologist: But they are not even looking at you, they are too busy with their own lives to even notice you.

Anxiety sufferer: I know that, but I'm scared they will hurt me.

Psychologist: Come on, no one is going to just walk up to you in the shop and hurt you for just being there. Everyone is entitled to go to the shop and buy what they need. People just want to buy their groceries and get home. No one is even concerned with you.

Do you see how this works? It seems a bit crazy, I agree, but this method really does work!

Emotional Freedom Technique (EFT)

EFT is the shortened version for the Emotional Freedom Technique.

It is also known to some as 'tapping.'

It was founded by Gary Craig in the 1990s, and since then has gone on to prove its worth for emotional and physical issues ranging from fear, anxiety, and depression to ailments such as multiple sclerosis, back pain, and even singing.

It is based on similar principles to that of acupressure or acupuncture, which aim to release blockages within the body's energy system. So instead of using needles, as is done in acupuncture, the fingertips are used in a tapping motion. The blockages within the system are believed to be what causes ailments, whether physical or mental.

During an EFT session, the fingertips are used to lightly tap on what is known as the 'end points' of the energy meridians on the body, all while saying positive affirmations and statements that are relative to the ailment.

Balance is achieved both physically and mentally as a result of the tapping and the saying of the positive and encouraging affirmation.

It is recommended that you visit an EFT practitioner, but you can also visit the following website http://www.emofree.com for more information on this interesting technique.

SIDE NOTE: *EFT should be done by a qualified practitioner so that you can get a full understanding of it before attempting it yourself.*

The 'RAT' Method

Recognise, Admit / Accept and Take Control is a method I devised myself taking inspiration from similar methods out there.

It is a fabulous technique when trying to see if you are just stressed out or if you are, in fact, anxious.

It is also good for helping those of you who are working on recognizing your symptoms and trying to accept your anxiety.

It will also help you to deal with the bad days more efficiently.

I promise you that I use this method often and it really helps me!

To explain this method better, I have put a brief example below:

Recognize – Take a moment to realize that you are stressed and anxious and to figure out what you are feeling. Are you angry? Are you nervous? Are you upset?

Admit and Accept – Say what you are feeling out loud as this will help you to accept it more easily. Be gentle with yourself and know that it's perfectly okay to feel emotional.

Take control – How are you going to better the situation? Are you going to do something about it? Or are you going to just let it go? This is the most challenging part, and for anxiety sufferers, we don't like anything upsetting our comfort zone.

So now let's look at a situation where this method would be used:

You just found out via the grapevine that someone who you like very much said something very hurtful about you behind your back.

'Recognize' that you are most probably hurt and angry. Allow yourself to feel these feelings.

The next step is to 'admit' and 'accept' that you feeling like this, because as we spoke about before, pretending that you 'don't care' is not going to help you in any way.

Then you need to 'take control.' You need to figure out what you going to do about the situation. Are you going to confront this person, or are you going to let it go and think of it as releasing a toxic person from your life?

Depending on what has happened or what your situation is, by the end of the second step 'Admit and accept' you should have been able to distinguish as to whether you are just stressed about something, upset or angry with someone or something, or whether you are indeed truly anxious!

This is why I love this method so much.

It not only helps us to work through our emotions rationally and in a healthier way, but it enables us to determine stress, anger or hurt from actual anxiety.

The example shown above is a very common scenario that happens to every one of us on a regular basis in various situations and areas within our lives, and these scenarios come with us having to make a choice. That choice being – how are we going to react?

You see, it took me so long to understand and realize that many of my reactions to occurrences in my life were making my situation worse.

Not that I'm saying that it's easy – oh boy, is it hard to try to make a healthy and rational choice when you are full of emotion.

Unfortunately, though, as anxiety sufferers, we do tend to overreact and stress ourselves so much over every situation that we lose sight of whether we are really having an anxiety attack, or if it's just a bit of stress. This method helps me with that!

Always remember that every choice has consequences, and that is just how life works, but we either make the right choice or we can learn from a bad one.

Cognitive Behavioural Therapy (CBT)

Cognitive Behavioural Therapy (CBT) is described as a talking therapy that helps to change how a person responds and reacts to thoughts and stressful situations.

It teaches you to cope with your anxieties, stress, and problems in a more positive and healthy way.

CBT has had a high success rate of helping people with mental disorders, especially anxiety and depression.

When I had CBT with one of my many therapists, she would ask me to write down something that had happened during the week that was stressful for me and how I responded to it. When I went for my session with her, she would then teach me how I could have responded to the situation in a more positive way that would have caused me less anxiety.

SIDE NOTE: *CBT needs to be conducted by a qualified and reputable therapist.*

Schedule Time To Worry

This is one of the most bizarre stress hacks I have ever heard of, and to be brutally honest, I was sceptical as to whether I should include it in this book or not. As far as I am concerned this technique is quite ingenious in some ways, and yes, it does work, however, it does have its negatives! So, the fact remains that you will have to try it out for yourself and see if it works for you or not.

Scheduling time to worry is actually one of the tools used in Cognitive Behavioural Therapy (CBT) and has been backed by research.

The whole idea is to set up a time and place every day (at the same time) to sit and worry. If and when worrying thoughts come up during the day, you should write them down on a 'worry list' to worry over later during your scheduled worry time.

It is incredibly hard to have a worrying thought enter your mind and try to not think about it, and naturally when someone tells us not to worry about something, we automatically do, (white bears experiment,) so rather than telling yourself not to worry, simply postpone your worry for your designated worry time slot and carry on with your day!

This technique is said to help you gain a certain amount of control of your worry and by doing that will allow for a smoother and more worry-free day!

Now here are the issues that I have with this technique:

First of all, as an anxiety sufferer, I can tell you that even when you tell your brain that you are 'postponing' your 'worry' or stress for later, it is still incredibly hard to switch off the worry and keep the intrusive thoughts from entering your mind.

Secondly, a lot of my recovery has been based on focusing on happy things, positive thinking, and the law of attraction, and I have spent a lot of time and effort (and still do) in trying to train my mind to simply acknowledge intrusive thoughts and then try to let them go and not dwell on them. Therefore, when I had my worry time, and I let the anxious thoughts consume my mind for 10 minutes straight, I found myself getting quite anxious because I didn't want them in my mind to begin with!

Thirdly, I wonder if doing this technique could make an anxiety sufferer even more anxious in the long run, by forcing themselves to worry for 10 minutes straight on a regular basis, when the whole point of recovery is to replace intrusive thoughts with positive thoughts?

However, on the other side of the coin, here are some positives that I found with this experience:

I found that sometimes, some of the things I 'worried' over made me realize that my so-called problems are really nothing but my own anxieties that are playing with my mind.

Also, even though it was a major struggle for me to 'postpone' the thought for the scheduled worry time, I honestly can say that I somehow felt better, knowing that I would get to worry about my problem later.

All in all?

You have to try this for yourself and make up your own minds.

As you can see, from my point of view, this technique has both positives and negatives, however, for me personally, I made the decision not to use it in my recovery plan, but I have included it in this book because it can, and has been shown to, work for many other people.

SIDE NOTE 1: *On that note, please look up The White Bears Experiment! It's interesting stuff!*

Interesting Extras and Important Information!

The following section is a list of six other alternative therapies that I came across in my research that were strongly recommended for treating mental disorders such as anxiety.

I have put these in a separate list to the other tips mentioned as unlike all the others, I have not personally tried these, however I have included them for a reason:

There are so many different therapies and treatments out there and we all respond differently to different things and this is why I am mentioning these to you. Perhaps you have exhausted all other avenues and you are looking for something different that may just be able to help your anxiety.

Please remember though, that if you wish to give any of these therapies a try, it is recommended to always fully research it and make sure that you get in contact with a reputable therapist.

Out of curiosity, I decided to do research myself and have included a bit of information on each of them below.

Psychodynamic Therapy

Also known as psychoanalytic therapy, this attempts to unveil the unconscious state within a person in order to help relieve stress, tension and negative feelings.

It is believed that sometimes when we experience anxiety, depression, or other types of distressing behaviours or disorders, that it may be our unconscious mind holding on to painful memories and emotions, so by bringing these emotions to the surface, a person can deal with the anxiety or stress in his/her conscious state better.

Psychodynamic therapy differs from hypnotherapy because hypnotherapy attempts to make suggestions to the person's unconscious mind in an effort to change certain behaviours, whereas psychodynamic therapy aims to bring deeply harboured feelings and emotions to the surface.

If you feel that you may want to try this specific therapy, please make sure you always find a reputable and qualified therapist!

Always do your research before you undertake any kind of treatment, therapy, or healing!

Gestalt Therapy

Gestalt Therapy was developed in the late 1940's by Fritz Perls.

By using a holistic (whole) approach, gestalt therapy focuses on the present moment, and aims to increase a person's awareness of their immediate situation by getting them to become fully mindful and understand all their thoughts, feelings, perceptions, behaviours, sensations, and beliefs for their current situation.

Two popular methods used in gestalt therapy are the empty chair technique and the exaggeration exercise.

The empty chair technique involves the person sitting across from an empty chair and then engaging in conversation with either themselves or someone else such as a partner or work colleague. The roles are then reversed and the person will then take the role of the person they were 'talking' to.

This helps the person become more aware of the situation.

The exaggeration exercise is when the therapist asks the person to repeat or dramatize a particular behaviour, such as frowning.

This helps to make the person more mindful of what feelings the behaviour brings about.

If you feel that you may want to give gestalt therapy a try, please make sure you always find a reputable and qualified therapist!

Biofeedback

This is a therapy that teaches you how to gain control over certain involuntary bodily functions. Think about how you do something without thinking about it, such as lifting your hand to scratch an itch or walking up a staircase – those are voluntary actions.

When we get scared and we start sweating and getting heart palpitations, those we don't have control over – these are involuntary actions.

Biofeedback involves attaching electrodes to a person's body in order to see how the rate of certain bodily functions, such as breathing and sweating, change when the body is under stress. The therapist will then help you to change these bodily functions such as improving your heart rate when it speeds up under stress.

Please seek out a registered and reputable therapist if you want to try out biofeedback therapy!

Magnet Therapy

Magnet Therapy is mainly used to relieve chronic pain, but it is gaining popularity for also helping those with depression and anxiety.

It involves placing magnets on specific areas of the body to relieve tension and pain.

It is thought that when the negative end of a magnet is placed on an area of pain, blockage or tension, the negative ions can help by encouraging fresh oxygenated blood to that area. Since magnets are also alkaline, it counteracts any acidity within that area.

Please seek out a registered and reputable therapist if you wish to give magnet therapy a try!

Please always do research to help give yourself a basic understanding of the specific therapy that you wish to try.

Hypnotherapy

I am quite sure you have all heard of hypnotherapy.

This involves a person being put into a deeply relaxed state and then listening to suggestions and ideas put forward by a therapist in order to improve problems, stress, or negativity within their lives.

As always, seek out a qualified and reputable therapist if you wish to give hypnotherapy a try!

SIDE NOTE: *Once when I called one of the anxiety help lines, the lady I spoke to was telling me how much hypnotherapy had helped her anxiety! We all benefit from different things, so it is always worth it to explore every option – no matter how silly it may seem!*

Tremor Release Exercise

Tremor or Trauma Releasing Exercise (TRE) is a series of exercises that help the body to release stress, trauma, and tension within the muscles.

It was created by Dr David Berceli, whereby the natural shaking and vibration mechanism in the body, when activated, helps to relieve muscle tension and enables the nervous system to calm down and return to a normal state of being again.

Dr Berceli founded TRE while working with people in Africa and the Middle East under traumatic war zone circumstances. He observed that when threatened, humans automatically start to shake or quiver. The TRE method is inducing this shake to get rid of stress.

TRE is backed up by research that says that stress and tension is relatable to both the physical and psychological forms. The vibrations and shaking that the body experiences are actually very soothing to the recipient and they feel very calm after a TRE session.

Although TRE is quite safe and natural, it should be done in a controlled environment with a TRE practitioner.

SIDE NOTE 1: *The following website will be able to help you further:* https://traumaprevention.com/

Noise Tips

Noise

Have you ever noticed in scary movies that as soon as something scary is about to happen, they add scary, loud music to emphasize the moment?

That is because it makes the scene more frightening and makes your adrenaline pump.

This is because certain noises aggravate, anger, and irritate us, and certain noises calm and soothe us.

This makes me think of the recent fireworks that have been going on with Halloween and Guy Fawkes Day.

Frankly – I can't stand it.

I become a ball of nerves, and I have to take rescue remedy and either put a movie on with the volume louder than usual, or put my earphones on, because every bang that goes off makes me jump.

Noise pollution has been linked with aggravation, aggressive behaviour, and increased anxiety.

In fact, there is a rare but very real phobia called 'phonophobia' whereby a person cannot tolerate loud noise and any anticipation of loud noise causes extreme stress and anxiety.

Noise pollution is very much increased in cities, where there are lots of cars, people, and shops.

If you live in the middle of a city centre, try these tips to escape the noise and into the quiet:

- Find the closest park and retreat there for some quiet time.
- Open your windows to let in fresh air during 'off peak' times and then shut them when the city is at its busiest.
- Create a peaceful ambience inside your living space. Light some scented candles and play some relaxing music. Another great idea is to get a miniature water fountain.
- Wear ear phones or ear plugs if there is bulldozing or construction going on nearby your house.
- Get soundproof glass installed in your windows.
- Move! Seriously, I know this may seem like a big step, but there are many people who have to move because of certain situations that are causing them ill health. Your

home should be your sanctuary, a place to come to and put your feet up after a long day!

Music

There are many musicians who have said that they can only express themselves through music, and music is what gets them through bad days, and I think we can all see why.

Everyone knows that music speaks to the soul and we tend to want to listen to music that fits in with our mood.

Opt to play light relaxing background music in your home instead of angry loud music and see what a difference it makes.

Of course, I'm not saying that you must never listen to loud heavy music again, but simply try to incorporate more "soul feeding" happy music.

In our house, we often have music playing in the background, and we choose very light relaxing sounds that will help and inspire us to get on with what we need to do for the day.

Some of my favourite music to listen to is:

- Nature sounds
- Celtic music
- New age music
- Instrumental music like harp or piano

Pink, White and Brown Noise

These noises are aimed at calming and relaxing a person in order to be able to sleep or even study.

They can sound similar at first but they do have differences between them.

They have proven to aid many people, especially those who struggle with insomnia and concentration issues.

Although, I personally prefer brown noise, my husband and I always have some sort of 'noise' playing softly when we sleep at night.

White noise is when sounds of different frequencies are combined, so the sound will play evenly on all audible frequencies. So, let's think of it as if you were to play a single note on a piano. White noise would be that single note, but it would be played on every frequency running from low to high that is audible to a human ear and combined into one "noise." You may ask, "How is it possible that a person can sleep with this playing at night?" When something is noisy, it's actually the irregularities that are in the noises or music that irritate us when we are trying to sleep. By reaching all the audible frequencies, white noise acts as a barrier and blocks out the irregularities that cause insomnia or annoyance. White noise sounds just like heavy rain or static.

Pink noise is also played on all audible frequencies, but the strength or power of the high frequencies have been turned down, making the lower audible frequencies stronger and louder. For those people who find white noise too harsh or annoying, pink noise may be a good alternative. Pink noise is said to slow and regulate your brain waves, thus aiding in sleep. Pink noise sounds to me like a gushing river or stream.

Brown noise takes pink noise a step further by turning the lower-frequency noises into more of a humming sound rather than pink noise's hissing sound. The depth of brown noise is said to aid in relaxation, promoting sleep. Brown noise sounds like a gushing river to me, only deeper. It is my favourite one out of the three.

SIDE NOTE: There are some amazing apps that you can purchase and/or download directly onto your phone or I-pad. We have 3 of them, and they all contain various tones with natural sounds like running water and bird life and many relaxing and calming pieces of music. The colour noises mentioned above and the isochronic tones that I speak of further in this book are also in some of these apps. You can also find many of these sounds on YouTube as well.

Time Management Tips

Planning Ahead / Routines

One thing about me is that I'm a very 'routiney' person. I like structure and I get very upset if my routine is disrupted. It drives my husband mad and we often have a giggle about it, but the truth is, it really helps my anxiety.

Funny enough, I never used to be like this. I was untidy, dysfunctional, and was often late for work or social engagements. When I was struck down with anxiety, planning ahead, being on time, and getting a diary really helped me to plan my life more efficiently, and let's face it, nothing is more distressing than always running out of time.

It still amazes me how I've managed to become the complete opposite of what I once was. Even when my parents came for Christmas, my Mom remarked, "When did you become so obsessed with colour co-ordinating your bathrooms?"

Okay perhaps, I'm still slightly dysfunctional ☺ but I promise you that making a simple to-do-list and being able to cross them out once I've done them is the most satisfying thing in the world!

Time management is also going to make your life a lot easier.

Aim to get to your appointments on time by always leaving a few minutes earlier than the time you should leave to account for getting lost (which I am famous for) or things you can't control, like bad traffic.

Even if you're not the busiest person in the world, having a diary can really help you to organize even daily chores. For example, I find a diary really handy to mark as to when I need to get my anxiety medication refills. I have had the misfortune of running out of them on more than one occasion and let me tell you it was not pretty!

Another thing that I find calms me down when I have a lot to do, is to aim to do a bit of everything each day. I don't know why it is, but I feel happier when I've managed to complete a bit of each task I had planned for the day, rather than completing only one task 100%.

I can't explain it, it's just how I cope better. I think it may be a psychological mindset in that if I've started the task, then I will have to complete it somewhere along the line.

However, if you are the type of person that likes to dedicate your time to one task until completion – then please by all means – go for it!

It's all about what works for you - and while we're on the subject of what works for you - something that I like to do is to plan my day the night before, and I will decorate the page to make it more visually appealing so that I am more inclined to do the tasks I have set out to do! I know it sounds weird, but I promise this really works for me!

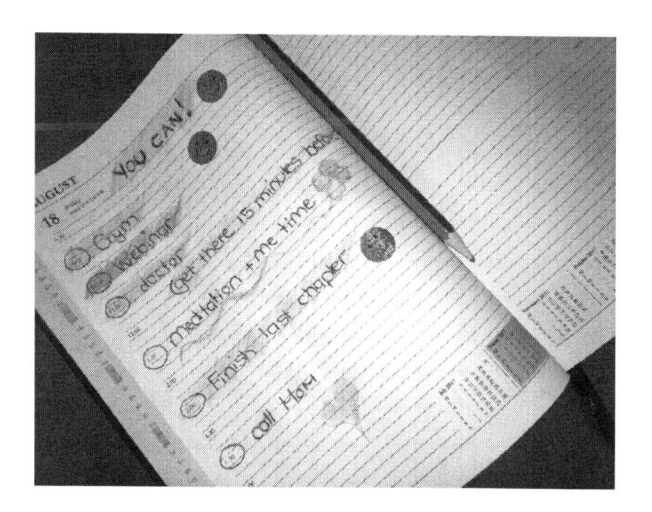

Image credit: Author's own

Adopt The 'Slow Down' Rule

Before we get into this tip, here's a little biology lesson for you ☺

We all have what is called an automatic nervous system which controls all things involuntary, like breathing or our heart beating.

This system breaks off into two others systems known as the sympathetic nervous system and the parasympathetic nervous system, and they work in the exact opposite of each other – meaning only one can be activated at a time.

The sympathetic nervous system is responsible for inducing the 'flight or fight' response in us, making us tense and wary, whereas the parasympathetic system relaxes us.

Anxiety disorder sufferers live in a constant state of anxiety, meaning that our sympathetic nervous systems are working in overdrive and our parasympathetic systems are working minimally.

In order to get the balance restored between the two systems, the parasympathetic system, in particular the vagus nerve, must be stimulated and we can achieve this by adopting a 'slow down' rule.

So, in theory, you want to slow down with everything you do in your life. One way is to eat very slowly, another way is to allocate some time for yourself to do something and add extra time onto it.

So, if you want to go for a 15-minute walk, make it a 30-minute walk.

One of my favourite ways to do this is to breathe slowly and deeply.

Whenever I consciously think about it, I will start to breathe more deeply and fully, enabling more fresh oxygen into my lungs and expelling all the stuck spent air that didn't exit my mouth when I was breathing shallow and quick.

You will really be surprised at how badly we breathe! We spend most of our lives breathing shallowly and not utilizing all the fresh air that we can.

Another tip I got which I like to combine with deep breathing through my nose, is to close my eyes and lightly touch my lips. This stimulates the parasympathetic nervous system instantly as the lips contain parasympathetic fibres which induce feelings of calm!

SIDE NOTE: *Previously I mentioned how blowing cool air onto your thumb can help to calm you down? This is because it also activates the parasympathetic nervous system!*

Tips for Stigma and Dealing with Shame

Know That You Are Not Insane

There is a hideous stigma attached to mental illnesses that spark up images such as people strapped to beds in a white padded room, and this is not true at all.

There is a big difference between being mentally ill and being mentally insane.

Most mentally ill people actually live normal lives. They go to work every day, have families, and live generally normal lives like anyone else.

Unfortunately, though, because it is a 'mental' problem, this means that it's to do with the mind, the head, or the brain, so immediately people assume that you are insane.

Just because you experience anxiety and nervousness on a much deeper level than other people doesn't make you insane! Again, think about it in physical terms. If someone has a deep scar on their leg from a car accident, do we automatically assume that they are disabled?

Do we assume that they can't walk or do normal everyday things?

A great technique is to say affirmations to yourself, such as "I am normal" or "I am still me" or "I am not my illness," just to start getting yourself to believe the fact that you are not crazy.

Don't Be Ashamed

Following on from the point above, you need to learn to not be ashamed of your mental illness, and the first step to achieving this is to not give in to believing all the crazy talk involving mental disorders.

Again, think of it like this: a migraine sufferer is not ashamed of their aching head.

A sinusitis sufferer is not ashamed of their sinus. So why should anxiety sufferers be any different?

It took me a while as well to really embrace this, but you have nothing to be ashamed of.

Do not - I repeat, do not, let society and stigma cast shame onto you.

Anxiety disorders are bad enough without having to deal with other people's ignorance. Unfortunately, you will meet people within your circle who will understand your condition and then people who won't understand, and you will quickly learn who will stand by you in your time of need and then those who run for the hills.

I have come across a few of these individuals in my life, and I immediately cut them out.

Stick to the people who will support you and who are worthy of your time and friendship. There is nothing worse than someone who treats you like the devil's spawn just because you have an anxiety disorder.

Just because some of us suffer with mental disorders doesn't make us any less deserving of being treated like a normal human being.

Getting To Grips With Your Anxiety

Admit When You're Feeling Down

One of the worst mistakes I made was trying to fight the fact that I was having an off day.

It took me 15 years to realize this, so now I'm saving you 15 years of waiting and I'm telling you this now.

Take it from me, it doesn't work to try brush the anxious feelings off. It will only leave you more exhausted and irritable.

They always say the first step toward recovery is admitting that you have a problem, right? Well if you're having a bad day or a bad week or even 3 bad months, just admit it to yourself. Trust me, admitting that you have anxiety is not giving in to defeat, and it certainly won't make your anxiety any worse.

In fact, it actually makes life a lot easier because you are telling yourself, "Hey, I am not feeling so good today," and this 'subconsciously' makes it okay and encourages you to practice self-care during the bad days.

Admitting to something is also not dwelling on the negative.

Dwelling on something is when you constantly think about the negative aspects of the issue. What I am telling you to do, is don't fight what you're feeling. Accept you are having a bad day and then fill your mind with happy and positive things.

We are taught to believe that we need to hide our feelings and constantly put on a brave face all the time!

Guys – honestly it is OKAY to have a bad day!

SIDE NOTE: Look at yourself in the mirror and say "I am not feeling my best today, and that's okay!"

Image credit: Pixabay/Antranias

Accept Your Anxiety

Never before has acceptance of something been more important.

This is my NUMBER 1 piece of advice for any anxiety sufferer!

You cannot even begin to recover from anxiety unless you have accepted it first.

They always say the first step to getting well again is to admit you have the problem, and how can you admit it when you haven't accepted it.

I always like to use the diabetes example when I'm thinking of things in the physical because it reminds me of a movie I watched that actually helped me to accept my anxiety.

The movie was of a daughter who was diagnosed with diabetes and after the doctor explains how the illness will impact her life, her mom turns to her and says that they will fight the illness. The nurse then turns to the mother and says, "You'd do better to make it your friend."

It honestly makes sense!

Don't fight it – accept it, and by accepting it, you become calmer within yourself and you can focus with a clear mind on how to alleviate the symptoms on the bad days.

I swear to all of you that accepting my condition has made SO much difference in my life!

It has helped me to get better! To know that I don't have to use every ounce of my strength to fight something that I can't even see is very rewarding.

You might be thinking, "But I have accepted it. I know I have an anxiety disorder." Maybe so, but think about how you react when those anxious feelings and symptoms come along. Do you sit and dwell on them, start to cry and do your best to fight them off? Or do you simply let them do their thing and concentrate on diverting your attention elsewhere by using one of the many tips in this book?

There is a big difference between knowing that you have an anxiety disorder and actually accepting that you have one. As I said, the real test is on how you react when the going gets tough.

How do you accept something as debilitating as anxiety? I have listed a few tips below:

- Read every success story that you can lay your hands on to equip your mind with the fact that anxiety can and does get better.

- I know this is hard but try to think about something you have gained from your anxiety: I promise that you may be surprised.
- Research! The more coping strategies and techniques that you have stored in your mind, the more second-nature it will become to you to utilize them and to spring into action before the symptoms get a chance to become bad.

Think of it in physical terms, like the girl with diabetes – do you think she could just ignore it and pretend it's not there?

Know Your Triggers

Being aware as to what triggers your anxiety can really be helpful so that you know your limitations.

Sometimes we get anxious for what seems like no reason at all, but actually there was something that happened during our day that may have triggered the anxiety.

That's okay, we will not be able to know every single one of our triggers, but if you do know of any, you can make your life a lot easier by avoiding them.

Triggers are a very personal thing as they are different for everyone.

What triggers me off may not trigger you off and vice versa. As you get better at managing your anxiety, you will learn what affects you and what you are okay with.

A lot of you may also be thinking, "Shouldn't I be facing my fears?"

This will depend on you.

It is different for everyone, and I will discuss this in the tip entitled "Do something you've always wanted to do but have been too scared."

It may even help you to keep a record of your triggers and how you handle the situation if and when you are unavoidably confronted with them.

Investigate and Research

There are so many different ways to approach recovery from an anxiety disorder, and what works for one person may not work for another.

We are so blessed to have a variety of knowledge right at our fingertips by means of the internet.

Get onto the net and research to your heart's content. Knowledge is power, and the more you research and read other people's stories, the more resources you have to try until you find something that works for you.

Never just diagnose yourself. If you suspect you have an anxiety disorder – make an appointment with your doctor and they will be able to either refer you to a psychiatrist or, at the very least, discuss treatment options with you.

Most doctors will discuss going onto medication.

Also remember that just because one doctor says so, it doesn't mean you have to go with their advice. Never feel pushed into going onto any kind of medication and if you don't feel comfortable, then go for a second opinion. Go for a third if you must. It is important that you understand what is going on with you!

Always remember that you are in charge of your own mind and body and it is vital that you feel comfortable with your treatment plan.

Once you have been diagnosed, and you are happy and comfortable with the doctor in question, then a good place to start is to first educate yourself on anxiety disorders, if you are not very clued up on them. Once you understand anxiety disorders better, start researching different ways that people have treated their anxiety disorders.

There is no one way to treat something, and anxiety disorders are no different.

There are natural ways, complementary ways, alternative ways, unorthodox ways, and the conventional medication way to treat anxiety disorders.

Explore all options!

I use a complementary way of treating my anxiety disorder.

Name Your Anxiety

My first book was called My Anxiety Companion, and I did this for a good reason.

In the book I talk about how I gave my anxiety a name, how I chose to ally with it, and how doing this is gave me the strength to accept it, which helped me to start on the road to recovery.

Naming your anxiety will also give a more playful outlook to the condition, which will make it seem like it is not such a big thing to have to cope with.

Making Life Easier

Survival Toolbox

A survival toolbox is kind of like a routine or a list of things that you can do daily or regularly to help keep you anxiety free, or at least keep the anxiety to a minimum.

A survival toolbox is so much more than just a list of things to do, and it is extremely important that you try stick to it.

It is exactly what it says: It is your survival list of things to do.

These are the things that you need to do every day, or at least regularly, to keep you stable and able to manage your anxiety.

In order to stick to your survival toolbox, list things that are easy to stick to, because these are going to have to be integrated into your current lifestyle!

For me personally, this was a bit of a lifestyle change for me and I just started doing these things every day until they became habit - because keeping my anxiety to a minimum was, and is still, that important to me!

So, think of a survival toolbox again in the physical terms.

Take a diabetic for example.

They would have to inject themselves with insulin and eat a diet that will help them as a diabetic. So that would be their survival toolbox.

To give you an idea, here are a few of the things in my survival toolbox:

- A relaxing positive meditation every morning – even if only for 10 minutes
- Saying what I'm thankful for every morning when I wake up
- Eating a healthy diet
- Regular exercise

Recovery Toolbox

A recovery toolbox is what you would refer to when you have a bad day or when you are going through a rough patch.

In order to do this, you must think of things that really help to alleviate your anxiety and what works best for you.

This book is basically your recovery toolbox 'list' to choose from.

Select what works best for you and create your own list.

Some of the things in my recovery toolbox include:

- Admitting when I don't feel so good and practicing self-care
- Watching a funny movie
- Watching a cartoon
- Taking some rescue remedy

Get A Support Structure

I really feel for those of you who don't have the support that you so desperately need, because it is a vital component to recovery.

If you have a trusted relative or friend who can support you whenever you need it, then grab that person with both hands. However, for those of you who are not that lucky, please don't despair – we've got you covered.

This is where mental health organizations and support groups come in very handy. The people there will listen to you without judgement or ridicule. They will comfort you and reassure you. They will hold you when you cry, and will listen with a willing ear.

All you have to do is check for mental health support in your country and area – there are so many of them. You can also check my website's 'Helpful resources' section to find mental health support in your country.

I have also included a few Facebook pages that are excellent at offering support and information. Please refer to section 2 for these.

Image credit: Pixabay/Anemone123

Think About The Big In The Small Term

I love this technique because it's helped me to really accept my anxiety for what it is.

When we are diagnosed with a hectic illness, be it physical or mental, we tend to go into self-denial, because we don't want to have this awful illness in our lives.

When I was first diagnosed, I was inconsolable. All I could think of was this horrendous illness that was so big compared to me. It seems like I was standing at the foot of a huge mountain that never seemed to reach the top – the mountain was my anxiety disorder.

This is where this technique is just the greatest! Instead of thinking of it in big terms, think of it in small terms.

I find what helps me to do this technique is to think of other people who have a chronic and/or deadly illness that really impacts their life.

For me, thinking of someone who could be worse off than me in terms of illness always helps me.

I tend to think of my anxiety disorder as being the smallest of the biggest, the best of the bad bunch.

In other words, anxiety disorder is an illness, and a very debilitating one at that, but as opposed to many other debilitating and often untreatable illnesses, anxiety disorder is treatable, and you can still live a really awesome and normal life once you have learned the tools to manage bad days with anxiety.

There are so many people who are dealing with the most unbelievable challenges right now. If you try and think about it like that, this technique works. Think of your problems as being smaller than they are.

Learn To Say No

Are you one of those people who feels guilty if they turn someone down?

If you are – you are not alone. It's not easy to say no, because it seems like we will be hurting people's feelings, but unfortunately it is vital for you!

People who suffer with mental illness need to keep their stress levels low and taking on too much will most definitely contribute to stress.

From a personal point of view, saying no has always been a challenge for me.

When I was younger, I thought people would not like me if I said no, and felt like I was letting them down. Now I can say no, but I'm still learning to not feel guilty about it.

How to say no:

- If the person has asked a favour of you that someone else can help with, perhaps suggest to them some names or contacts of those other people who could help. It will soften the blow and will make them feel better about you saying no.
- If you get invited out somewhere and you're not up to going, tell the person that you can't go on that night, but you would love take a rain check and have them over for a coffee at your place. This immediately will make them realize that it's not because of them that you don't want to go out.
- The word 'perhaps' or 'but' are very good words to make use of in these situations because it offers the person something more than just a flat-out no. Such as: "I cannot take on any more work right now, but I will help you with any questions you may have," or, "I won't be able to give

you a ride to the station tomorrow, but perhaps I can on Friday?"
- Be honest. When all else fails, be honest with the person and tell them that you not up to going out because you're feeling anxious. Perhaps your boss asked you to take on another project. Simply tell them that you are snowed under with other work and cannot take on anything more right now.

Keep It Simple

You know how some people say, "I love a challenge," well I'm going to be one of the opposites of those and say that I don't like a challenge – well, too much of a challenge that is.

It winds me up and sets off my anxiety.

Of course, this doesn't mean that I don't face challenges in my life, but rather that, if given the choice, I would prefer to keep my life simple and uncomplicated.

This is not because I am lazy, or because I don't believe in hard work, but because I am a recovering anxiety sufferer and I prefer to be smart about it.

Why overcomplicate things when you don't need to? An anxious mind is already complicating every single thing in life so why add to it?

Simplicity is something that I try to live by every day because by keeping things within your life simple, it helps to keep your mind simple. It's really as 'simple' as that! ☺

Your anxious mind doesn't need the added stress!

Don't make things harder or trickier than they have to be.

Obviously, it cannot always be avoided, and we all have to work hard to achieve what we want to, but just remember that, 'within reason,' when you can, keep it simple!

Always remember than less is sometimes more.

Occupy The Mind

My Mom once told me that someone she worked with said to her one day that she had to work, otherwise it made her depressed and anxious.

This makes a lot of sense.

Keeping the mind busy will prevent you from dwelling on your anxiety.

Sometimes lying about the house with nothing to do is the worst thing for anxiety sufferers, so if you don't work or are unable to work, you need to try keep yourself busy, or else take up an activity that you enjoy, or get involved in volunteer work.

If you do feel an attack coming on, for whatever reason, do something to alleviate it.

You could do one of the many tips mentioned in this book. You could phone a friend, watch a movie, bake, or garden. You could put on some music and dance or sing.

The possibilities are endless.

SIDE NOTE: *Meditations are also brilliant for anxiety attacks. YouTube has plenty of different meditations that you can try. I would suggest going through some that you like and saving them into a playlist. I also have a few meditations on my YouTube Channel that you can try.*

Stay In The Moment

Easier said than done, but don't worry about the future.

Now I don't mean this in the sense of not having dreams and goals. I mean try not to foresee or worry about 'what ifs' in your future.

Dream big and don't worry about the how, just focus on believing that your dreams will come true!

Just take one day at a time, especially when you're going through a bad patch, and concentrate on making each day the best that you can do, not what other people perceive as the best, but what you perceive as the best. If your best means getting out of bed, getting dressed, and going to the shop on your own, then so be it.

Worrying about the future only adds more stress to your life. Honestly, no good comes from worrying – says me who never stops worrying, but it really is so true.

I can tell you that I have personally had to force myself to do this.

Four years ago, when my husband and I immigrated to the United Kingdom, I was so homesick that I honestly was suicidal. I wanted to go back to South Africa and I grew increasingly depressed with every passing day. My husband left for work very early and worked in London and got home very late at night. I knew no one, and I found England to be very different from South Africa.

I would sit at the top of the stairs with my dogs crying my eyes out, not knowing what to do, and then one day, I had an epiphany.

I just knew that I had to give it time, and that in the end everything was going to work out fine.

From that day on, I continued to struggle along with getting used to the British way of life, but I focused on filling up each and every aspect of my life with happy and positive things.

My depression lifted because I honestly believed that everything would be alright in the end. (Shout-out to epiphanies!) ☺

Here we are four years later, and my belief came true.

We live in a new beautiful house near a gorgeous park and both my husband and I are truly settled, and we know that the UK is our home now.

Even the dogs seem to love it now ☺

So, stay in the moment.

Take each day as it comes, and when you can't take each day, then take it hour by hour, even minute by minute, if you must! As soon as your mind starts to wander and worry about tomorrow, divert it back to today!

Sleep Tricks

Get 8 Hours or More of Sleep a Night

This is a pretty obvious one, right? Lack of sleep makes us lethargic, moody, irritable, forgetful, and emotional. The problem is that many people who suffer with anxiety disorder have insomnia as did I at one stage! So, I completely sympathize if you are one of these people.

So here are my top tips for insomniacs:

- Try to not sleep during the day. Even if you are tired, get up and do something to stop you from going to sleep. It is important that your body clock 'resets' itself and knows that night time is for sleeping and day time is when you should be awake. However, if you do need a short nap, average for no longer than 30-45 minutes.
- Install a red or amber light in your room or else decorate your lamps with red lampshades. The red colour will help to create warmer tones in your room and help make you sleepy.

- Do not under any circumstances drink caffeinated drinks at night. Caffeine is a stimulant and will cause your heart rate to speed up, thus causing adrenaline to be pumped around your body, sending you into the fight or flight mode, which is the state in which your body is reacting to danger and is getting ready to either flee the situation or stay and fight it.
- Get yourself one of those night time teas from a health shop. They are made from herbs that will induce sleep and are designed to help you relax as well. They are also free of caffeine.
- Switch off all electronics at night. The light from electrical devices disrupts melatonin release, which is your sleep inducing hormone. They also keep the brain active because of the increase in electrical activity within the brain and speeding up of neurons. It is a good idea to do what you need to do on your cell phone or I-pad, and then shut it off for the night.
- Eat something starchy at night. Starch, such a baked potato, raises our serotonin levels, making us feel relaxed and calm.
- Get an old stocking and place some **fresh** lavender flowers inside it and hang it close to where you sleep. Lavender

has long been praised for its relaxing and sleep inducing properties.

- Listen to isochronic tones. These are regular beats of a single tone to induce sleepiness by stimulating the brain to what is known as "brainwave entrainment." In simpler terms, you can think of a sound that is being turned on and off at an extremely rapid rate.
- Listen to binaural beats. These can be used in conjunction with isochronic tones and is when two different sounds are played into the ears, one sound for each ear. The brainwave pattern will then "make up" or "play out" the difference between these two tones. So, if the tone in your left ear is 100 hertz (Hz) and the one in your right ear is 105 Hz, then the difference will be 5 Hz, your consciousness will automatically hear the 5-Hz brainwave. Binaural beats require headphones and are amazing at inducing a sleepy state.
- Listen to monaural beats. This is when beats are made up into one complete sound before we hear them. For monaural beats, the sounds must be the same for each ear. These, on their own or combined, have been proven to improve the brain's chemistry, thus reducing stress, anxiety, insomnia, improving concentration, and even aiding in studying.

- Another option you have is to listen to brown, pink, or white noise. Please see the hack entitled Pink, brown and white noises.

SIDE NOTE: *Both my husband and I have experienced great benefits from the tones, beats and noises, and we cannot sleep without one of them playing in the background. I suggest you listen to each of them and decide which one works best for you. My favourites are the binaural beats and the brown noise, or else a plain nature sound such as raindrops.*

Weighted Blankets

This was a new one for me!

A weighted blanket is a type of blanket that moulds onto the body like a snug fit. The deep pressure from the weights in the blanket brings about a sense of relaxation and a feeling of safety. Think of a hug – it's the same effect!

When gently applied to the body, pressure encourages serotonin production – serotonin being our happy and calming hormones. The weight of the blanket gently puts pressure on the body and stimulates the production of serotonin, which converts to melatonin, which are our sleep hormones.

Weighted blankets are proving to really help people with a variety of problems including anxiety, depression, autism, and insomnia.

The weight recommended for an average sized adult is between 15-30 pounds (7-15kg.)

Weighted blankets can be very expensive, but you can also make them yourself if you feel like a bit of DIY.

If you're not sure whether you will take to a weighted blanket or not, I would suggest in the winter months try adding one of those thick heavy blankets over yourself and see how you cope with that first!

Do Not Nap For More Than 45 Minutes

I suffer from mild CFS, due to a really horrendous viral infection that I had years ago, so if my body calls for a time out, then I will go and have a lie down.

A lot of people think of taking a nap as lazy, but if you think about it logically, the average person only sleeps 6-8 hours a night, therefore leaving 16 hours that we are awake and on our feet, busily going on with our lives.

In fact, in Spain it is very common for people to take a siesta during the day and in Japan it is a sign of working hard if you take a nap.

When it comes to how long you should nap for, I personally would say anything from 20 – 45 minutes, but no longer. If you nap for longer than 45 minutes, you start to enter the deep sleep pattern which will result in you feeling as though you've been dragged through a bush backwards when you wake up.

We go through 5 sleep stages when we sleep, including REM (Rapid Eye Movement).

Stage 1 is when we nod off. It is light sleeping. Our eyes move slowly and it is here that we can also experience that 'falling' feeling when we suddenly jerk awake. Our brains will also produce what is known as alpha and theta brain waves.

In **stage 2** our eyes stop moving and brain waves become slower. If you were to take a short powernap, it is here that you would want to wake up.

Stage 3 is when our brains produce delta waves, which are very slow waves. There is no muscle activity.

In **stage 4**, only delta waves are produced, and the body starts to repair itself and prepare you for the next day ahead. It is difficult to wake someone up in this stage, which is why we feel very groggy if we do wake up here.

In **stage 5,** which is the REM stage (Rapid Eye Movement,) our breathing becomes short, fast and shallow. The eyes move in all directions and heart and blood pressure is increased. This is where we begin to dream. The brain is obviously very active in this cycle.

You enter REM about 90 minutes after first falling asleep and one complete sleep cycle is roughly between 90-110 minutes.

Helping Others To Help You

Talk It Out

Some people advise against talking about your feelings and your anxiety because it makes you focus on them, and I can understand why they would say that, but there is a fine line between talking out a problem and confiding in someone on a bad day, and completely making anxiety your whole life, thought process, and conversations with people.

So please understand the difference between these two things.

Talking out your issues is sometimes the best thing you can do.

There is nothing better than the other person responding to your fears and then being able to give you the reassurance that everything will be okay.

Sometimes a big old hug and hearing someone else confirm that 'it will be ok' just makes you feel so much better.

They might even be able to suggest something to help you that you haven't thought of yet.

If you do not have someone to talk to, then please pick up the phone and call one of the mental health support centres in your country – that is what they are there for.

Donate Your Time

I am not just talking about donating unwanted items here.

You can donate anything that could help others.

You could help out at soup kitchens or volunteer to walk dogs at animal shelters.

Perhaps you would like to donate some money or help raise funds.

You could do litter picking or give blood, read to the elderly or sick children. Any cause that is close to your heart, you could donate your time to.

It not only helps others less fortunate, but you as well!

It creates a good feeling inside because you're helping others and you're creating a karmic energy. When we give, we receive – it's just how it works.

For me personally, I fostered puppies for animal shelters. I hand reared puppies as young as 10 days old and it gave me a whole new lease on life!

The Best Things In Life Are Free

Laughter Is Truly The Best Medicine

This is such a fantastic way to relieve anxiety, and it is by far one of the easiest things to do! Whenever I am sad, I will go and watch something funny on TV or on YouTube.

Whether in TV form, book form, or joke form, I don't care, but just laugh until your sides hurt.

For all the spiritual people out there, did you know that when you laugh, you automatically raise your vibration to sync in with that of the earth's energies?

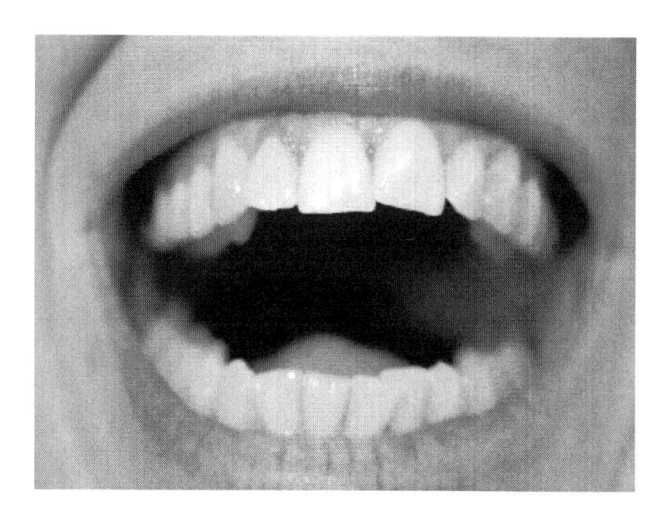

Image credit: Pixabay/Kjerstin_Michaela

Give Yourself Me Time

Practicing self-care has never been so important before.

People who suffer with mental illness often start hating themselves and loathing everything about their physical and mental being because they are ashamed of having a mental disorder.

Self-care and taking some time for you will help to diminish these feelings of self-loathing.

You deserve to take some time out! You deserve to love and be loved!

There are hundreds of ways to practice self-care. Just think of things you enjoy, but don't always get to do.

Just a heads up: This does not mean that you have to actually do something.

If giving yourself 'me' time is about lying in a hammock outside and staring at absolutely nothing in particular – then that is fine. This is about YOU and what you want to do in your 'me' time.

See below for a few self-care ideas:

- Switch off the technology for 30 minutes! Switch off your phone, switch off the TV, and switch off the computer. Go and lie down somewhere comfortable and just stare into space! If it's a nice sunny day, go stare at the sky! Just stare, rest, and just be!
- Do something you enjoy. Whether it is reading a book, baking, gardening, dancing, singing, playing a computer game, or watching a movie. Dedicate 30 minutes to doing only this and avoiding everything else.
- De-clutter - Spring clean your home and donate unwanted goods.
- Have a candlelit bubble bath.
- Buy yourself a new outfit!
- Take a nap.
- Go sightseeing. If you are like me, I love going to museums and tourist attractions. I find it very soul soothing.
- Go to a day spa.
- Organize a coffee date with a friend.

Spread Love

Helping others makes us feel good and, once again, it creates that 'what we give out – we get back'.

This tip doesn't only relate to giving to charity though. It could be the smallest thing to make someone's day better.

You could smile at someone or you could help someone carry stuff to their car. Perhaps you saw someone drop something – pick it up for them.

Just treat people how you want to be treated!

Nature

I think almost everyone knows the powerful effect that nature has on a person's soul.

Almost all the meditation videos that I have seen place a nature image into the video.

However, just what is it that makes nature so incredible?

Here are a few reasons to help us understand it better:

- Oxygen is abundant in nature because trees are what supply us with it. Inhaling all that oxygen and fresh air helps to regulate our serotonin levels (serotonin is our feel-good hormone). It also helps the blood pressure.
- As mentioned previously in the Himalayan salt lamp tip, nature can only emit negative ions which help to relax us and clear the mind and body. Remember positive ions are emitted from electronic devices like TV's, radios, cell phones, and computers – anything that is electrical, which make us stressed and irritable.
- Even on a cloudy day you can get a bit of Vitamin D, and vitamin D helps the absorption of calcium. Calcium is an anti-stress mineral.
- When you are exercising outdoors, you are creating endorphins, which make you happy, and combined with the fresh air, this allows for a cleaner and happier mind and body.
- Nature is so pretty. No matter what the season, I always find it beautiful, whether its summer and spring with its gorgeous flowers, the oranges and reds of autumn or the lovely whiteness of the snow in winter – it's always beautiful. We have become very 'city' dependant human

beings. We are indoors a lot and children prefer to play video games rather than ride their bikes or play by the river. Maybe it's because nature is simply 'natural' and it reminds us of the simple things in life without the 'busyness' of our modern lifestyles.

Image credit: Author's own

Water Tricks

Hold An Ice Block When You Feel A Panic Attack Coming On

This hack is literally at your fingertips because we all have ice in the fridge.

Hold one ice block in one hand for as long as you can and then transfer it between hands or you can put it in a small tea towel.

The coldness of the ice will literally snap you away from your anxious thoughts and make you focus on the coldness in your hands.

When we have a panic attack, or we just feel stressed, our bodies go into 'flight or fight' mode and adrenaline is pumped through our body, causing symptoms such as sweating and hot flushes.

Using the coldness of the ice, you can also help to ease the heat your body produces during these attacks.

Suck On Ice Cubes Or Frozen Vegetables

If you're one of those people who likes to eat when they get nervous, or even if you're merely a person who likes the feeling of chewing gum when you're stressed, this one is for you! This is also a great tip for summer time.

Sucking on an ice cube creates the same action and feeling as chewing on gum or food, but without the fat and added sugar. I do recommend popping a few ice cubes in a glass of water and let them shrink in size a bit before you start sucking on them!

For a really fun twist, try adding a squirt of fresh lemon, lime or orange juice when making the ice blocks.

My personal favourite however, is to sit with a bowl of frozen peas and corn and suck and chew on those. It's such a great boredom buster as we also tend to want to chew when we are bored. It's also a great stress reliever, and it's healthy.

Cold Water Shocker

Everyone knows that when we are in shock over something bad that has happened, or we are super stressed or anxious, someone will say 'go and splash some cold water on your face,' but how and why does this work so well?

All mammals have a reflex known as the mammalian diving reflex, (also called the immersion reflex,) which is activated when our faces touch cold water.

This reflex is utilized in diving when divers jump into the cold water, but the same principle applies when you put cold water onto your face.

What it does with the divers, is it helps them to breathe with decreased levels of oxygen, so it helps to stay under water for long periods of time.

When this reflex is activated, it decreases the heart rate and blood pressure. It also narrows the blood vessels, reducing blood flow to our limbs, thus allowing more blood to reach the heart and brain.

That is the whole science behind it, but now I will present my own 'unexperted' opinion as to why I enjoy this hack.

When I'm about to splash handfuls of cold water on my face, I usually take a deep breath in. I think it's that automatic response to covering your face with your hands and psychologically thinking I won't be able to breathe properly while the water is on my face – who knows, it's weird, but I do.

By taking this deep breath, it immediately stops my quick shallow panicked breathing for a few seconds.

Secondly the shock of the cold water will snap you back into reality.

SIDE NOTE: *This trick works very well to help you feel more energized in the morning!*

Wash Your Hands In Warm Water

For me personally, I've always used the hot water tap when I wash my hands.

The warm water soothes me, even in the summer months. It has always been a natural automatic thing that I've done.

Lately though, I started to think maybe there is a reason why my body responds to it and low and behold – there actually is a reason! I discovered that, once again, the parasympathetic nervous system is involved.

The warmth of the water engages the calming effect of the parasympathetic nervous system which is responsible for slowing our heart rate - cool stuff hey?

SIDE NOTE: *I would like to encourage you all to look up the parasympathetic nervous system and get a basic understanding of it. It's really interesting reading, and there are other ways to activate it to enhance the calming soothing effects.*

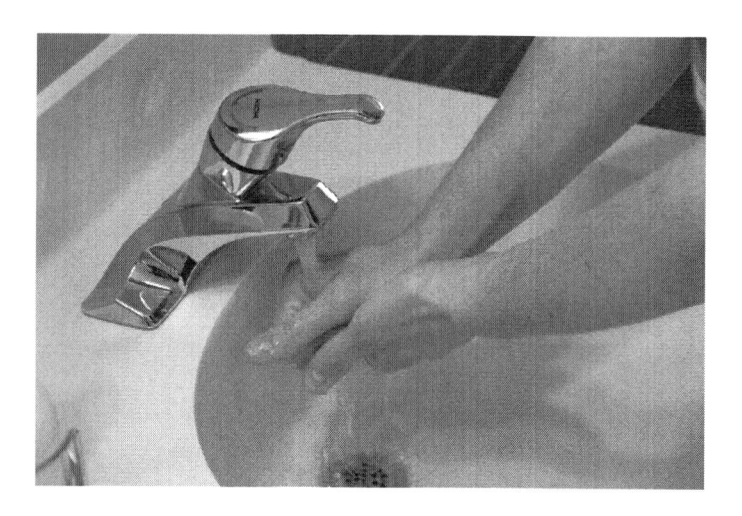

Image credit: Pixabay/offthelefteye

Challenge Yourself

Do Something You've Always Wanted To Do, But Have Been Too Scared

Just like there is a fine line between talking out a problem sometimes and having your anxiety monopolize every conversation, there is also a fine line between facing a fear or trigger and doing something you've always wanted to do but have been sceptical.

First of all, a fear or a trigger is something that you don't like, that you don't want to associate yourself with, and it triggers anxiety within a person.

There are absolutely no positive, happy or excited feelings that go with this.

However, wanting to do something because you think it may be fun and exciting, but being a little nervous about it, is a completely different story.

So, for example – I would never ever go to something like the London dungeon because I know that it will instantly set off a panic attack, however I've always wanted to get a tattoo, and as excited as I was about it, and as much as I knew that I would love my chosen design afterwards, I was really nervous about having the procedure done!

However, once the artist started tattooing me, I realized it wasn't nearly as bad as I thought it would be!

What I am saying, is don't put yourself in 'panic attack' situations, but challenge yourself to do something fun, new and exciting – maybe you will feel a bit apprehensive about it, but you will look forward to it as well. ☺

Section 2 – Helpful Resources

Facebook Pages:

Wounded Butterfly

Ups and Downs in the USA and UK

Mental Health and Invisible Illness Resources

Let's talk Mental Health now

Inspiration, Truth, Love and Life

Mental Health Inspiration and Information

Dissociative Identity Disorder Devon

SIDE NOTE: Don't forget to "like" the My Anxiety Companion Facebook page ☺

Books:

Self-help for your nerves – Dr Claire Weekes

From Panic to Power – Lucinda Bassett

The Linden Method – Charles Linden

The Secret – Rhonda Byrne

Anxiety Support Centres:

Anxiety support centres, counsellors, and support groups are all over the place. There are actually just too many to mention, and they are situated all over the world. To find an anxiety support centre near you, your best bet would be to either do an internet search or else ask at your local doctor's office.

If you're not keen on support groups or talking to someone on the phone, then I would suggest an online support group. Here you would be in the comfort of your own home behind your computer, and you won't have to see anyone or verbally talk to anyone face to face.

I do have the names of some support groups and helplines by country, on my website. Check out my **Helpful Resources** section on www.myanxietycompanion.com

Section 3 – References and links

Exercise Recommendations

5 benefits to doing Legs up the wall:

http://www.doyouyoga.com/5-health-benefits-legs-wall-posture/

Eating and Diet Reminders

Is decaf coffee good or bad https://authoritynutrition.com/decaf-coffee-good-or-bad/

Decaf coffee and health

http://teeccino.com/building_optimal_health/39183/Decaf-Coffee-And-Health.html

Vitamin B 12

http://www.naturalnews.com/032766_cyanocobalamin_vitamin_B-12.html

Lifestyle Reminders

Smoking and mental health https://www.mentalhealth.org.uk/a-to-z/s/smoking-and-mental-health

Natural Medicine

St John's wort

https://en.wikipedia.org/wiki/Hypericum_perforatum

Relaxation Hacks

Salt Lamps and Anxiety http://www.higherperspectives.com/salt-lamps-1979583022.html

Salt lamps fight anxiety and depression http://www.healthiestalternative.com/science-proves-himalayan-salt-lamps-fight-anxiety-depression/

What is colour therapy http://www.colourtherapyhealing.com/colour-therapy/what-colour-therapy

Simple self-care practices http://tinybuddha.com/blog/45-simple-self-care-practices-for-a-healthy-mind-body-and-soul/

Why nature is so relaxing http://mentalfloss.com/article/60632/11-scientific-reasons-why-being-nature-relaxing

How to ground yourself http://www.evelynlim.com/how-to-ground-yourself-in-7-ways/

Ear massage

http://thehealthylivinglounge.com/2010/03/29/teach-yourself-8-of-the-best-ear-massages/

Ear massage for stress http://www.onsiteplus.com/stress-ear-massaging-spot-benefits/

How to slow down

https://www.psychologytoday.com/blog/turning-straw-gold/201109/4-tips-slowing-down-reduce-stress

Stress tips http://www.healthista.com/10-ways-to-deal-with-stress-and-anxiety-youve-never-heard-of/

Blow air onto your thumb http://www.sun-gazing.com/apparently-blow-air-thumb-happens-body/

Weirdest stress hack ever

http://www.newsweek.com/career/weirdest-stress-reducer-ever-totally-works

Fractals https://www.psychologytoday.com/blog/codes-joy/201209/fun-fractals

The Naam Yoga Hand Trick

https://alternativeyoga.wordpress.com/2017/08/15/stress-relief-in-the-now-an-instant-stress-relief-series-naam-yoga-hand-trick/

101 ways to destress https://www.ditchthelabel.org/101-ultimate-ways-chill-reduce-stress/

Psychology Methods and Therapies

Tremor Release Exercise http://traumaprevention.com/what-is-tre/

Cognitive Behavioural Therapy http://www.mind.org.uk/information-support/drugs-and-treatments/cognitive-behavioural-therapy-cbt/#.WB3BQk1vhl8

Cognitive Behavioural Therapy http://www.nhs.uk/conditions/Cognitive-behavioural-therapy/Pages/Introduction.aspx

Psychodynamic Therapy http://www.counselling-directory.org.uk/psychodynamic-therapy.html

Psychotherapy https://www.bpc.org.uk/about-psychotherapy/what-psychotherapy

Difference between hypnotherapy and psychotherapy https://franzblauhypnosis.wordpress.com/2012/03/08/what-is-the-difference-between-hypnotherapy-and-psychotherapy/

Gestalt Therapy http://gestaltcentre.org.uk/what-is-gestalt/

Gestalt Therapy http://www.goodtherapy.org/learn-about-therapy/types/gestalt-therapy

Gestalt Therapy http://www.counselling-directory.org.uk/gestalt-therapy.html

Gestalt Therapy http://www.psychologycampus.com/psychology-counseling/gestalt-therapy.html

Biofeedback https://www.mayoclinic.org/tests-procedures/biofeedback/about/pac-20384664

Acupuncture and Magnet Therapy http://universityhealthnews.com/daily/depression/two-alternative-therapies-for-improving-anxiety-depression-symptoms/

Noise Tips

6 ways to deal with noise http://www.mnn.com/health/fitness-well-being/stories/6-ways-deal-noise-pollution

Time Management

Time Management http://bargainbabe.com/living-with-anxiety-one-simple-life-hack-sane/

Sleep Tricks

Weighted Blankets http://www.mosaicweightedblankets.com/anxiety-disorder/

Weighted Blankets http://www.lifehack.org/351993/sleeping-with-weighted-blankets-helps-insomnia-and-anxiety-study-finds

Sleep Cycles https://sleep.org/articles/what-happens-during-sleep/

Understanding sleep https://www.ninds.nih.gov/Disorders/Patient-Caregiver-Education/Understanding-Sleep

How long should you nap https://sleep.org/articles/how-long-to-nap/

Napping Guide https://www.theguardian.com/lifeandstyle/2009/jan/27/napping-guide-health-wellbeing

How gadgets keep you awake https://sleep.org/articles/ways-technology-affects-sleep/

The Best Things In Life Are Free

Reasons to smile http://www.mindbodygreen.com/0-7693/smile-5-reasons-it-will-make-you-happy.html

Fake smiling

https://www.forbes.com/sites/rogerdooley/2013/02/26/fake-smile/#6691a9a36765

Smiling reduces stress http://www.smithsonianmag.com/science-nature/simply-smiling-can-actually-reduce-stress-10461286/

Using your non-dominant hand

http://www.nwitimes.com/niche/shore/health/using-your-other-hand-benefits-your-brain/article_6da931ea-b64f-5cc2-9583-e78f179c2425.html

Using your non-dominant hand

https://www.goodfinancialcents.com/benefits-of-using-your-opposite-hand-grow-brain-cells-while-brushing-your-teeth/

Using your non-dominant hand

https://www.today.com/money/afraid-flying-try-writing-your-name-wrong-hand-t112671

Scheduling worry time https://healthypsych.com/psychology-tools-schedule-worry-time/

Should you schedule time to worry

https://www.mindbodygreen.com/articles/should-you-schedule-time-to-worry

Water Tricks

Mammalian Dive Response

https://www.breatheology.com/articles/mammalian-dive-response/

Mammalian Dive Reflex

https://en.wikipedia.org/wiki/Mammalian_diving_reflex

Splash cold water on your face

http://www.lesaviezvous.net/science/why-splashing-cold-water-on-your-face-relaxes-you.html

About the Author:

Mel Bonthuys experienced her first anxiety attack in 2001, but was only officially diagnosed with anxiety and panic disorder in 2008.

Throughout the many years that Mel spent suffering, she finally got on the road to recovery and is now an advocate for mental health, spending her time helping others find hope and happiness again!

When she is not writing books or blogs, she is making mental health videos, or spending time with her husband and their two rescue dogs.

She currently lives in England.

You can get in contact with Mel via her website:

http://www.myanxietycompanion.com/contact-me.html

It would be very much appreciated if you would leave a review of this book either on Amazon or Goodreads.

Other Books by Author

MY ANXIETY COMPANION

My journey with my mental illness ... a story of hope and inspiration.

MEL BONTHUYS

To purchase My Anxiety Companion, please click

http://www.myanxietycompanion.com/book.html

Printed in Poland
by Amazon Fulfillment
Poland Sp. z o.o., Wrocław